Java™ Gems:
Jewels from *Java Report*

SIGS REFERENCE LIBRARY

Donald G. Firesmith
Editor-in-Chief

1. Object Methodology Overview, CD-ROM, *Doug Rosenberg*

2. Directory of Object Technology, *edited by Dale J. Gaumer*

3. Dictionary of Object Technology: The Definitive Desk Reference, *Donald G. Firesmith and Edward M. Eykholt*

4. Next Generation Computing: Distributed Objects for Business, *edited by Peter Fingar, Dennis Read, and Jim Stikeleather*

5. C++ Gems, *edited by Stanley B. Lippman*

6. OMT Insights: Perspectives on Modeling from the Journal of Object-Oriented Programming, *James Rumbaugh*

7. Best of Booch: Designing Strategies for Object Technology, *Grady Booch (Edited by Ed Eykholt)*

8. Wisdom of the Gurus: A Vision for Object Technology, *selected and edited by Charles F. Bowman*

9. Open Modeling Language (OML) Reference Manual, *Donald Firesmith, Brian Henderson-Sellers, and Ian Graham*

10. Java™ Gems: Jewels from *Java*™ *Report*, *collected and introduced by Dwight Deugo, Ph.D.*

11. The Netscape Programmer's Guide: Using OLE to Build Componentware™ Apps, *Richard B. Lam*

Additional Volumes in Preparation

Java™ Gems:
Jewels from *Java Report*

COLLECTED AND INTRODUCED BY
DWIGHT DEUGO, PH.D.

dwight@objectpeople.com

PUBLISHED BY THE PRESS SYNDICATE OF THE UNIVERSITY OF CAMBRIDGE
The Pitt Building, Trumpington Street, Cambridge CB2 1RP, United Kingdom

CAMBRIDGE UNIVERSITY PRESS
The Edinburgh Building, Cambridge CB2 2RU, UK
http: //www.cup.cam.ac.uk
40 West 20th Street, New York, NY 10011-4211, USA
http: //www.cup.org
10 Stamford Road, Oakleigh, Melbourne 3166, Australia

Published in association with SIGS Books & Multimedia

© 1998 Cambridge University Press

All rights reserved.

This book is in copyright. Subject to statutory exception and to the
provisions of relevant collective licensing agreements, no reproduction
of any part may take place without the written permission of Cambridge
University Press.

Any product mentioned in this book may be a trademark of its company.

First published 1998
Reprinted 1998

Design and composition by Barbara Crawford
Cover design by Brian Griesbaum

Typeset in Calisto

Printed in the United States of America

A catalog record for this book is available from the British Library

Library of Congress Cataloging-in-Publication Data is available

ISBN 0-521-64824-6 paperback

Introduction:
Java Report in Review

JAVA REPORT published its first issue in March 1996. At that time, Sun had spun off its Java development group into a new business unit called Java Soft, headed by Dr. Alan Baratz. Many developers were avoiding their real jobs and using Java to enhance their homepages. Important members of Sun's Java team had left to form their own companies. Moreover, helping to drive the Java market into the mainstream were the growing numbers of new Java IDE vendors, training companies, component builders, bookstores—the leading technologies are always the ones with books taking up the most shelf space—and the growing army of Java converts. Java, the language developed by Sun initially for programming electronic appliances, was gaining mind share at an incredible pace.

In his first editorial for *Java Report,* David Fisco wrote:

> "The Java community is becoming broader ever day, encompassing CIOs, information technologists, market professionals, programmers, multimedia designers, educators, managers, and even hobbyists. . . . However, many CIOs, developers, and even software experts are having a hard time getting a handle on Java. Some have said that it's just a neat way to run animations on the Web, others note that Java enables Web-based electronic transaction, and still others tout Java as the Holy Grail that will bring about the $500 PC and change the world of computing as we know it."

There was much hype surrounding Java. It had collected the right combination of buzzwords to describe itself: simple, object-oriented, distributed, interpreted, robust, secure, architecture neutral, portable, multithreaded, and dynamic. The reality was that those words reflected features

v

vi INTRODUCTION

that provided solutions to a diverse set of problems faced by many different individuals and corporations involved with software development.

Today, to state the obvious, Java is pervasive. The number of people reading about and trying out Java is enormous. JavaOne, Sun's Java conference, had over 10,000 attendees this year. There have been over 400,000 downloads of JDK 1.1. Another indicator of Java's popularity is the number of books on the topic. When was the last time you read about a programming language in the newspaper? Java just keeps showing up everywhere. It is safe to say that there are hundreds of thousands of people now involved with Java, with that number expected to grow continually.

Java, the little language that could, has grown into a language that can. It is now poised for use in building mission-critical Internet/Intranet and standalone applications for the enterprise. Company after company is making the switch and the commitment to objects and to Java, a decision that I believe is the correct one for today's business and software challenges.

Java Report's mission from the very beginning has been to be the independent, objective source of information about Java. Its intent is to inform, enlighten, and entertain. Initially a bimonthly publication, after its third issue it was evident that the magazine would have to follow the growth of Java and it changed its publication schedule to ten issues per year. Its page count also increased from 64 in the first issue to 80 in the latest one. This year, with the release of JDK 1.1 and 1.2 not far off, Java continues to grow in functionality and use. To keep pace, *Java Report* is doing the same. For 97, *Java Report* has changed to a monthly magazine as well as increasing the number of pages. Will anything derail the growth of Java? Provided it continues to deliver on its promises and people use it correctly, Java has a very bright future. *Java Report* has and will continue to help technical managers and developers use Java correctly by providing up-to-date information on topics and issues that they will face immediately and in the near future.

Officially named as editor-in-chief in May, although I had been working on various issues since January, I succeed the founding editor-in-chief—David Fisco. David had one of the hardest jobs anyone can have in publishing: establishing a new publication and developing its readership. Although the task was difficult, David directed *Java Report* through its first ten months to become the leading Java publication. One might say that since the topic of the magazine is Java, the hype alone will lead to success. However, I argue that people will only read and recommend a magazine they find interesting and informative, one that continues to focus and enhance its quality. The last point is important. There are many competing companies in the Java market, from product vendors to service organizations. I believe the industry will see a shakedown towards the end of 97 or early 98, and the winners will be the ones with an emphasis on quality. Being first to market helps one generate market share, but quality is what keeps it! David continually increased the quality of the magazine throughout last year, adapting it to meet changes to Java and to meet the needs of you, the reader.

If you read the anniversary issue of *Java Report,* you found me there as the guest editor. This was a test issue for me—not primarily for SIGS to see if I could do the job, but for me to decide if I wanted to do it on an ongoing basis. Being an editor involves performing a number of different tasks with a diverse set of people. You talk with people about submitting material, read and comment on the material, and check the proofs of accepted articles. However, that is only for the technical features. I read every issue before its publication for any problems and for my own information—yes, even I learn from *Java Report.* I also meet with companies or visit their homepages to keep informed of what they are doing and to know about what they plan to do next. There are also product reviews to schedule, people who want to talk with you for whatever reason, and that other major task I have: Director of Java Services at The Object People. You do not think you can be the editor of a technical magazine without actually working with the technology, do you?

At any one time, I am dealing with three different issues. There is the issue that just hit the streets—I am talking with people about its contents. There is the issue that is in production—I am checking that for quality. Then there is the next issue—I am looking for good articles for the issue's theme. Thanks to your submissions, the number of quality articles available for publication is growing. I also try to convince colleagues and leading members in the community to write for *Java Report.* It may take a while to get them to agree, but I can be a very convincing person.

Getting someone to say he or she will write an article is often easier than getting them to complete the article. You would be surprised at how long it takes some people to write a 2000–3000 word article and at the excuses for not doing so. I know everyone is busy. If you are not, you must have a problem. However, the problems and issues that you are dealing with are ones of great interest to a number of people in the Java community. Hundreds of thousands of people are new to Java and to object-oriented programming. If you have discovered, developed, used or

viii INTRODUCTION

solved something interesting relating to Java, write about it. The pattern community has learned the benefits of this. What will it take to convince you to do the same?

Java Report is written for and by colleagues in the Java community. Only you know the problems, solutions, details, and issues that are important. For example, you know why your Java projects succeed or fail. You know the types of projects being developed. Only you can help to keep *Java Report* continually focused on your needs. Aimed at knowledgeable Java users, feature articles explore some area of the language, such as ways to use Java effectively, traps and pitfalls, novel uses, or arguments for and against particular language features. Articles containing descriptions of particular commercial products are normally excluded. In addition, in each issue an expert group of columnists explores in detail a particular aspect of Java. Each issue provides detailed book and product reviews, corporate profiles, one-on-one interviews with industry leaders and Java gurus, product announcements, and a survey of current trends in the industry

It was clear from JavaOne this year that Java is becoming a language not only for Internet application development, but also for enterprise application development. This is the next logical step for Java. However, it seems that every week I talk with a company that has a group of developers with no Java or object-orient experience that is going to build and deploy Java application this year, usually within the next three months. Java has, or will have, everything you need for software development. However, software development is HARD! Both the people and the language need time to mature. People need to learn the language and its features and what it's like to develop an object-oriented application: collaborating, cooperating, message-passing system. Java just needs to work out the kinks, although I will be the first to admit that the quality of 1.1 is very good.

Do you need to know all of Java's APIs to build an application? No. You only need to know about the ones you require. Java and its APIs are becoming analogous to the world's largest hardware store. When you want to build something, you go to the store, get the components you require and put your project together. The success of Java, like any good hardware store, depends on the availability of top quality, reusable components. This year Sun is filling the store with components. It is up to you, the builders, to put the pieces together. *Java Report* is your guide for this activity.

Java Report in Review   ix

This collection covers the last twelve issues of *Java Report,* from March 1996 to June 1997. Selecting articles proved difficult since *Java Report* had presented a wide range of interesting articles on different themes in that time. Themes have included multitasking, VRML and Java-Script, multimedia, getting ready for 1.1, database solutions, security, real-world Java, components, networking, reliability, AWT, and patterns to name but only a few. In addition, columnist's themes have included the Java Insider, Pragmatic Programmer, Madison Avenue Java, Practical Patterns, Business Objects in Java, Scott's (Java) Solutions, Java Means Business, The Database Connection, Graphic Java, The Java Tutor, Getting Started with Java. In all, *Java Report* has included 47 technical, feature articles and 57 articles from regular columnists, plus news, product evaluations, and company and book reviews that were not appropriate for inclusion in this collection. My task was to select 20 articles. I found it analogous to being in a candy store with only a dollar and wondering where to start. Excellence alone was not a sufficient criterion for pruning the 104 articles to my target number. I used the following criteria to base my final decision:

1. *Developer as intended reader.* I decided to not include any piece whose primary focus was business or managerial concerns, with the possible exception of David Moskowitz's piece, "Java Training Without Getting Soaked." Therefore, for example, I did not include articles by Tig Tillinghast, such as "Developers as Management Consultants," or by Joel Scotkin, such as "Visualization: How Java Can Add Real Value." Both regular *Java Report* columnists continually provide relevant insights into what managers need to know about Java. However, I wanted this collection to offer insights into Java for the developer.

2. *Relevant issues for today's developer.* With the changes and additions made to Java over the last year, I decided not to include any piece that was dependent on releases of Java before 1.1. This meant, for example, that pieces that used Java's old AWT event model did not make it into the collection, such as Henry Wong's article "A Look at Event Handling." I also wanted the topics addressed by the collection to match the concerns and issues of developers today.

3. *Not readily available from other sources.* I also decided not to include introductory material easily found in most sources. This meant that an

x INTRODUCTION

article such as Philip Meese's on "Creating Your First App" was not included. *Java Report* has a number of introductory pieces on API and techniques. However, many Java books deal with these topics at great length. If your bookshelf is not already filled with these types of books, I am sure it will be soon. Using the above criteria, my first pass through the back issues left me with a list of 40 articles—twice as many as I required. I was proud of the quality of the articles I had selected and of *Java Report* for its content, realizing it was going to be difficult to get that number to 20. On my second pass, I arranged the articles into sections relevant for today's developers and from that managed to get the number down to 30. Finally, I set a goal of no more than two articles per section and pruned the number of articles to 21. I could cut no more! I had not reached my goal, but I felt that to cut any more would take away from the overall flow of the collection. With a little persuading, Rick Friedman, the founder and publisher of SIGS Publications, agreed to revise the final number of articles, and the collection was complete.

The collection has nine sections: Introduction to Java, Language Features, Java vs. C++, AWT, Patterns, Techniques, Distributed Computing, Persistence, and Lessons Learned.

The collection begins with an "Introduction to Java," and it is only fitting that the first article is by an important member of the initial Java development team: Arthur van Hoff. Arthur was a Senior Staff Engineer at Sun. He was with Sun for three years and was involved in the development of Java since 1993. He was the author of the Java compiler, and was the HotJava project lead. Arthur's article, "Believing the Hype," examines what it will take to make Java successful. Hype may get a language started, but it is not enough to sustain its growth. Although written for the first issue of *Java Report,* the points made in this article are still relevant today. Java must attract a large following. It must help bring the Internet to the average consumer. Java must find its way into electronic devices. The Internet's bandwidth must increase. Java must continue to evolve and it must be fast.

Security is very important issue for Java developers, and an issue they must deal with from their introduction to Java. The fact that an Applet cannot freely access any part of the host system may be frustrating to some, but it saves many users from aggravation. As an example of what can happen when there is no security, at this year's JavaOne conference Sun demonstrated how dangerous downloaded Active-X components can be. Would you like your financial records opened and modified or your hard disk erased? I though not.

Applet access exemplifies only one type of security in Java. Joel Scotkin, a regular columnist for *Java Report,* examines other Java's security layers in his article, "Accessing the Java Security Layers."

There are a number of language features enabling Java to be used for more than just toy applications. This is evidenced this year by the fact that many companies are either using or considering Java as their language of choice for enterprise application development. The collection's "Language Feature" section includes three of those features: multitasking, interfaces, and a collection of features that enable Java to support I18N, also know as internationalization.

Distinguishing itself from other languages, multitasking is part of Java. As Barry Boone puts it: "Multitasking is not an operating system hack." Barry is the author of *Java Essentials for C and C++.* His article, called "Multitasking in Java," introduces threads and helps you understand when and how to coordinate them. In addition, Barry goes on to discuss deadlock avoidance.

The next article in the section is by Desmond D'Souza. Desmond is known within the OO community and writes a regular column in the *Journal of Object-Oriented Programming.* In his "Design and Modeling Opportunities in Java," Desmond discusses what interfaces represent and the opportunities they present for design and modeling to define behavioral types. The distinction between a type and a class is an important one in OO programming. This article helps you understand the difference.

The final article in this section is by Rex Jaeschke. In his "Java Goes International," Rex examines the features of Java that are used to support internationalization, that is, to build an application that has no dependency on any culture. For business applications and Applets, internationalization is extremely important. One does not want to restrict their application to use in only one language or in one time zone. Why do business locally when you could be doing it worldwide?

Java has included many features from other languages. For example, it was not the first to use a virtual machine; Smalltalk has been using one for years. Why has Java gained a larger base of users than Smalltalk? After all, Smalltalk is a purer object-oriented language—everything, including Integers, is an object. There are many reasons, but certainly one of the contributing factors is Java's similarity to C++. As James Gosling

xii INTRODUCTION

pointed out in his OOPSLA 96 keynote: we have to give C++ developers something better, but not a language that is so different from C++ as to make it impossible for them to make the switch.

The next section in the collection, called "Java vs. C++," contains two articles comparing the languages and their use. For those of you moving from Java to C++, Robert Martin's article, "Java and C++: A Critical Comparison," provides you with an unbiased comparison of C++ and Java. As he points out:

"I want to make it very clear this is not a diatribe against one language or another. I happen to like both Java and C++ quite a bit. . . . This article is simply a discussion of the differences between the two languages."

Barry Boone's article, "C++ vs. Java Software Development," makes a different comparison. This article examines how Java's features affect the software-development process—from design to maintenance—from a C++ perspective. If you have not switched to Java already, this article provides you with some compelling reasons to do so.

One area of Java that has gone through substantial changes in release 1.1 is the AWT. A number of articles and books have covered the AWT's new event delegation model. Moreover, with the addition of the Java Foundation Classes, the number of available components for GUI construction is continually growing. However, developers still have many questions not answered by the introductory material found in books.

To help with those questions, the collection's "AWT" section contains two articles by regular columnists of *Java Report:* David Geary and Henry Wong. David's article, "Answering Frequently Asked AWT Questions," discusses a few of the most frequently asked questions from comp.lang.java.programmer, such as how to access a component's frame and how to force a layout. Henry Wong's article, "Life Span of an Applet," examines what goes on in an Applet from its creation to its destruction. Both of these articles go beyond simply describing how to assemble AWT components. They discuss how specific components' behavior, such as that of an Applet, affects their operation

One of the most import contributions to software design was the book of *Design Patterns* by Gamma, Helm, Johnson, and Vlissides, also referred to as the Gang-of-Four. One of the reasons why it was important was because it popularized patterns. Developing complex object-orient systems is difficult. When you start developing a new system, are you really starting from scratch? No. Even if one believes the argument that there is little reuse of classes from one system to another, I argue that one does achieve reuse. In other words, you make use of your past experiences. Therefore, you should be better at developing your next system. Reading literature and attending lectures on patterns helps you achieve the same result without going through the struggle of developing a new system. You benefit from experience of others. More importantly, learning about patterns is a cost-effective method of enlarging your development skills. It is only fitting that Erich Gamma's article, "Applying Design Patterns in Java," leads off the collection's "Patterns" section. In this article, Erich reviews the different types of patterns and then discusses how the developers of Java have applied some well-know patterns to the AWT.

Iseult White continues the theme in her article, "Patterns and Java Class Libraries." In this article, Iseult describes how the Iterator and Factory patterns are implemented by Java in classes.

The final article in the section is by Allen Benson and myself. Our article, "Singleton," describes the Singleton pattern and provides an example implementation of its application.

Patterns are for everyone to know and use. If you have not yet started to apply patterns, let these articles be your introduction. However, I suggest you learn more. You and your system will benefit from the wisdom contained within them.

The next section I have titled "Techniques." Java provides you with a number of features and APIs. However, it is up to you to combine and use them appropriately to develop an application or provide new functionality. In this section, I have chosen three articles that provide examples of techniques derived from Java and JavaScript.

The first article, written by Jeremy Sevareid, describes a design for drag and drop which is common to ones found in other languages that provide the same facility. In addition, Jeremy provides a sample implementation using Java's AWT library.

The second technique is from Henry Wong's article, "Exception Handling: More Than Just and Add-On Feature." Henry's article compares Java's exception handling with C++'s. It goes further than just describing exception handling by defining some rules to help simplify using exceptions and without interfering with other mechanisms related to the exception system, such as threads.

Although many developers are using Java to develop Applets, many people are also imbedding JavaScript in their HTML pages. Since there

xiv INTRODUCTION

are several books on JavaScript, I decided not to include a section on it. However, as the third technique, I chose an article describing how to make JavaScript interact with a database. The article, "Tapping the Power of JavaScript" by Steven Disbrow, demonstrates that JavaScript is "not only good for creating those crawling announcements on the status line of the browser or for creating a clock that tells you the time." You can also use it with other Web tools to manipulate data on your Web pages.

Up until the introduction of Java, the typical enterprise applications had PCs communicating with a database client accessing a server—a standard two-tiered client-server application. However, with Java and the Internet, developers are now required to become familiar with other architectures, frameworks, designs, and patterns, for three-tiered client-server applications. For many, distributed business applications are a necessity, not a choice. In the section named "Distributed Computing," I included two articles to help developers with their transition to the third tier—which sometimes brings tears to their eyes!

Radha Bandarpalle and Raj Ratnakar's article, "Distributed Business Applications Using Java: An Implementation Framework," begins the section with a discussion on the three stages in the evolution of customer access to services and products of an enterprise. It then goes into a discussion on the advantages and disadvantages of sockets and CORBA for implementing the three-tiered client-server models.

Adam Feeman and Darrel Ince's article, "The java.net Library," completes the section with an implementation of socket-based client and server and a set of guidelines for applets and applications involved in client-server applications.

Most, if not all, Java applications require some form of persistent storage. Accepting this assumption, you must know how to make your data persistent, which, working with an object-oriented language like Java, means you must know how to store objects. As a Java developer, you have several existing options available to satisfy this requirement. In the collection's "Persistence" section, the first article by Patrick O'Brien, "Making Java Objects Persistent," looks at the strengths of four approaches: serialization, persistent storage engine, JDBC, and object databases, and describes where each option is applicable.

The section's second article, "StoreTable: A Java Class for Simple Object Persistence," written by Robert Howard, introduces StoreTable, a Java class that builds upon Java's serialization mechanism. As Robert states:

"The reason that using serialization for persistence is only appropriate for lightweight persistence is that it generally requires that an object be saved or recalled in its entirety. This is counterproductive for small updates to objects with many complex links to other objects."

Robert's StoreTable, a persistence-storage engine (PSE) without some of the more advance capabilities mentioned in Patrick O'Briens article, like transaction management, provides a simple, yet cheap, PSE. It solves the problem of using serialization by using a persistent hash table. It also provides a good example of where a class like the StoreTable, invented in Eiffel, can be translated to Java.

I called the final section of the collection "Lessons Learned." I could have included a number of articles in this section, but I decided to choose two pragmatic ones. Lowell Kaplan's opening sentence to his article, "Upgrading You Web Site to Java: The First Step," states a reality that Java developers will have to deal with when building their client-server applications:

"There is a lot of hype about what Java can do to improve a Web site; however, most sites still use HTML and CGI."

Lowell's article describes how a Java Applet can call a CGI program, send it parameters, and receive the results. He also describes a migration path for moving an HTML/CGI Web site to one that has Java on the front and back ends.

The collection's final article deals with an issue that I believe is important for the success of Java: training. It is not enough for you to know the syntax and semantics of the language and its APIs. They are important, but you must also understand how to build object-oriented applications. Training should help you develop the required skills. If we as a community fail at using Java to build successful enterprise applications this year and next, we will put Java's use in jeopardy.

David Moskowitz's article, "Java Training Without Getting Soaked," discusses how to make training work for you. As different people within an organization have different educational needs, David shares his criteria for successful training sessions and examines some of the myths of training. If you believe you know all there is to know about Java, you are wrong. There is always something new to learn.

xvi INTRODUCTION

After reflecting on my task of selecting and introducing the articles in this collection, I have one regret. I wish that I was not limited as much by space. *Java Report* has been fortunate in having an excellent group of writers and columnists from its conception. However, no one person represents its voice—it is their collective voice that makes the magazine a success. When one attempts to dissect that voice, there has to be a change in tone. The change in tone for this collection is the focus on the developer. Please realize that *Java Report* is more than what you read here, so I encourage you to pick up an issue to hear the complete choir.

The future looks bright for Java. Once the browsers and the IDEs catch up to the latest release, you will have vendor support, language support, and your company's support for Java application development. The rest is up to you. Do it right!

Our goal for *Java Report* is to help you do it right. We want to keep you informed of the latest developments and products in the industry. We want to help you learn and use Java's new APIs. We want to provide you with tips, techniques, and patterns for Java. We want to help you understand Java and object-oriented programming issues, provide answers to difficult questions and provide you with solutions to problems you will encounter. We want to help you and your projects succeed!

To help us achieve our goal, we need to hear from you. We need to know why your Java projects succeed or fail. We need to know the types of projects you are developing. We want your help keeping *Java Report* continually focused on your needs. *Java Report* is committed to you in being your premier source of information on Java. In return, I want to hear your views and any contributions you would like to make.

DWIGHT DEUGO, PH.D.
Editor-In-Chief
Java Report

Contents

Introduction: *Java Report* in Review   *v*

SECTION ONE • INTRODUCTION TO JAVA

Believing the Hype   *Arthur van Hoff*   *3*
Assessing the Java Security Layers   *Joel Scotkin*   *11*

SECTION TWO • LANGUAGE FEATURES

Multitasking in Java   *Barry Boone*   *19*
Design and Modeling Opportunities in Java   *Desmond D'Souza*   *33*
Java Goes International   *Rex Jaeschke*   *41*

SECTION THREE • JAVA VS. C++

Java and C++: A Critical Comparison   *Robert C. Martin*   *51*
C++ vs. Java Software Development   *Barry Boone*   *69*

SECTION FOUR • AWT

Answering Frequently Asked AWT Questions   *David Geary*   *81*
Life Span of an Applet   *Henry Wong*   *95*

SECTION FIVE • PATTERNS

Applying Design Patterns in Java   *Erich Gamma*   *105*
Patterns and Java Class Libraries   *Iseult White*   *115*
Singleton   *Dwight Deugo and Allen Benson*   *123*

xviii CONTENTS

SECTION SIX • TECHNIQUES

How to Drag and Drop Images *Jeremy Sevareid* *131*
Exception Handling: More Than Just an Add-On Feature
  Henry Wong *139*
Tapping the Power of JavaScript *Steven W. Disbrow* *147*

SECTION SEVEN • DISTRIBUTED COMPUTING

Distributed Business Applications Using Java: An Implementation
  Framework *Radha Bandarpalle and Raj Ratnakar* *157*
The Java.net Library *Adam Freeman and Darrel Ince* *165*

SECTION EIGHT • PERSISTENCE

Making Java Objects Persistent *Patrick O'Brien* *183*
StoreTable: A Java Class for Simple Object Persistence
  Robert "Rock" Howard *203*

SECTION NINE • LESSONS LEARNED

Upgrading Your Web Site to Java: The First Step
  Lowell Kaplan *215*
Java Training Without Getting Soaked *David Moskowitz* *223*

Section One

Introduction to Java

Believing the Hype

Arthur van Hoff

I T WAS LITTLE MORE than a year ago when the 25 members of the Java project team retreated for a brainstorm meeting to the Rickey's Hyatt in Mountain View, CA. Java was still young (only three years old), we had done the first Internet release, and we were starting to plan the product roll-out. The focus of the discussion was going to be the strategy for making Java and HotJava a success.

We spent two days in a conference room hashing out ideas and eating stale bagels. During the meeting we decided what would have to happen before we would consider the year to be a success. We decided that if Java was successful we would have 10,000 users, and 100 applets by the end of 1995. Little did we know our expectations would be wildly exceeded!

Four months later at the Solaris Developers Conference, Marc Andreesen walked on stage and announced Netscape's intention to support Java applets by the end of the year. We had heard rumors that there would be an announcement that day, but it was really exciting to be in the audience and get such a strong endorsement from Netscape. Only one year after our Hyatt meeting we have 15,000 people on our mailing list, hundreds of thousands of Java enthusiasts, and many commercial partners, including Microsoft, IBM, and Netscape. Java is clearly here to stay.

INTERNET FOR CONSUMERS

Today there are millions of users on the Internet. Most of these users are computer-literate PC users, and not the average consumer. As a result,

4   INTRODUCTION TO JAVA

most items sold over the Internet today are music CDs, comic books, and pizza.

Is this the future of the Internet?

The growth of the Internet is enormous, and every week thousands of new computers are added. Until now the growth has been exponential and many are starting to fear that this growth can not continue. Where will it stop? At the current pace everybody on the planet will have an IP-address by the end of the century. The growth has to slow down, and the number of connected users will slowly level off. But will the exponential growth stop once every existing PC and workstation is connected? That point will soon be reached. But besides finding more people that need computers there is another way to grow: find a way to connect people that don't need computers!

I don't believe that everybody needs (or wants) a PC running Windows 95. I know from personal experience that it is simply too expensive and complicated to own such a system without a reasonable understanding of computers, operating systems, and hardware. Instead of connecting more PCs, I believe that other categories of devices will be connected to the Internet, thus creating new markets and new opportunities. Some existing devices that are obvious candidates for Internet connectivity are cell-phones, pagers, fax-machines, palm-top computers, TVs, and anything else with a CPU.

INTERNET DEVICES

In addition to hooking up existing devices, several companies (including Sun) are building low-cost Internet access devices. Sun's device will be built to run Java applications, and will come bundled with the HotJava browser. The price of such a device has been estimated at $500, but to be realistic it will initially be much higher.

By the way, the total system price is really determined by the screen technology. It is still very expensive to create high-quality LCD screens in volume.

The biggest advantage of a Java Internet device is the low maintenance cost. The machine comes with a pre-installed Web browser, and additional software is automatically downloaded by visiting Web pages. The cost of such a machine will be a fraction of the maintenance cost of a PC. This is mainly because there is no need for software maintenance, since the software is administered centrally. This makes the Internet devices a very attractive option for large corporations who want low-cost end-user machines with centralized software distribution.

ELECTRONIC NEWSPAPERS

At the WWW4 in Boston, Bran Ferren from Disney predicted that in the future newspapers won't just disappear, they will be banned! Any printed material that is intended for one-time use will be illegal once we understand the environmental implications. I believe he is right: Printed books will not disappear, but newspapers and magazines will. An electronic newspaper has many advantages over the printed version. It is simply a matter of finding the right form factor and price point for the newspaper device.

In Japan, many palm-top devices without keyboards that do excellent handwriting recognition are becoming available. It is simply not possible to create a portable device with a Japanese keyboard. These devices are ideal for Internet connectivity. The failure of the Newton is probably due to its lack of connectivity and poor handwriting recognition. Palm-top devices with improved screen technology and wireless ethernet are ideal as Internet access devices and could replace the printed newspaper.

INTERNET BANDWIDTH

Another factor in the growth of the Internet is the available bandwidth. There is still a lot of dark fiber out there and we can expect an enormous growth in bandwidth. Bandwidth is a commodity and its availability is driven by market economics. As a result, the bandwidth will scale with the Internet.

A researcher at NASA explained to me once that their Virtual Reality engine was capable of doing only ten frames per second, even after many years of research. Every time the computers got faster, they simply added more polygons to the world so that the frame rate remained at a constant and only barely acceptable ten frames per second. The same thing is likely to happen with the Internet bandwidth. If there is more of it, you will also need more, making your applications always painfully slow.

So what will we do with the abundant bandwidth? What are the new applications? The Internet will be used more for real-time communication. Internet telephony and real-time video will become a reality once there is enough bandwidth. Wouldn't it be cool if you could be sitting in a cof-

6 INTRODUCTION TO JAVA

fee shop, make a phone call using your wrist watch, and browse the net using an electronic newspaper? Or is that already possible?

Once there is plenty of bandwidth, it will be possible to offload data from your machine onto the network. This lowers the cost of the devices and offers us almost infinite storage capacity. Storing data on the network will require the use of digital signatures to ensure the user's privacy. Today there are already similar services using the telephone network that provide storage space for voice-mail and fax messages.

THE ROLE OF JAVA

The Internet is clearly evolving to a much more interactive and much more consumer-oriented environment. Java plays a key role in this evolution. It enables the introduction of new small devices that run Java. Java allows the distribution of applets and applications to a wide variety of devices, and it makes the Internet truly interactive. But the Internet is too complicated for consumers. Have you ever tried explaining the concept of a URL to someone who has never used the Web? It is simply too abstract, too computercentric, and too complicated. It has to get simpler. We need applications that make the Web easier, not harder. We need applications for consumers.

The Java technology itself is very developer focused, but it enables a new class of applications that can hide the complexities and diversity of the Web. This is where the real future of the Web lies, a universal and easy-to-use interactive information network for consumers. That all existing software has to be rewritten in Java is an opportunity, not a problem. It is an opportunity to consolidate vendor-specific APIs and create a universal operating system that provides high-level functionality to applications. The APIs created for Java should be open, vendor-independent, object-oriented, and multi-threaded. That way every developer can benefit from them.

LANGUAGE EVOLUTION

What lies ahead for Java? Guy Steele and Bill Joy are currently finishing the Java 1.0 language specification, which will be published in book form this spring. We like the language as it is, and we anticipate very few changes in the near future. The language is simple and elegant and we would like to keep it that way. We should learn from C++ and not make the mistake of adding many features that each add very little value. A language that evolves too fast is hard to implement. Our objective is to enable stable and consistent implementations on all platforms.

Sun intends to stay in control of the language definition in the near future. Eventually it may be in our best interest to hand the language definition over to an independent standards organization, but we are worried that this will open the door to a flood of new features that will destroy the spirit and simplicity of the language. However, some language extensions have been considered as possible candidates for future version of Java. We've talked about adding parameterized classes to the language (similar to C++ templates), but again, we are very concerned that this would make the language much too complex.

Possibly the most requested feature is operator overloading. This is an emotional issue—some people love it and some hate it. Although it adds some expressiveness to the language, it also makes the language more obscure, and there is a never-ending debate on which operators are overloadable and which are not. I would vote against adding operator overloading and from what I hear it is very unlikely that this will be added in the future. Most of the innovation can be expected in the Java libraries and not in the language itself. There are plans for adding libraries for persistent objects, 3D graphics, video, audio, Web browsing, and so forth. We are very interested in evaluating third-party proposals for new APIs.

PERFORMANCE

Besides changes to the libraries, there are many other important improvements that we expect to make in the near future. There are many ways the performance of Java can be improved. I'm confident that Java will be as fast, or perhaps even faster, than C or C++ in a few years. Java interpreters can certainly be made to run a lot faster than they do today, but the Holy Grail of performance lies with native code generators. Currently several projects inside and outside Sun are underway to develop code generators for Java and the results are promising; a speed up of 10–20 times can be expected, putting Java in the same range as unoptimized C code. Although Java programs are statically compiled, there is still a need to do some runtime checking. In particular, null pointer checking, array bounds checking, and runtime type checking can't be done at compile time. This makes Java programs more robust, but it also makes the generated code a little slower than the equivalent C program. However, many of these checks can be eliminated at runtime by the native code generator.

8 Introduction to Java

It is possible that in the near future Java programs will run faster than C or C++ programs. The programs you run on your Windows 95 machine are compiled for the 386 instruction set. That means that these programs don't use any of the new Pentium instructions that your machine can execute. Also, the compiler has optimized the code for the wrong CPU. This means that the average Windows 95 program is only using a percentage of the potential power of your Pentium computer. A Java program doesn't suffer the same penalties. If you have a 90-MHz Pentium with 250-KB processor cache, the native code generator will generate machine instructions for exactly that CPU. Because the code generator knows exactly how much memory you have, how big the processor cache is, and how many instruction pipelines there are, it can generate much better code.

But that isn't all: it should be possible to make Java even faster by doing runtime analysis of the code. This and the structured nature of the Java language allow for many optimizations that are not possible in C programs. We are also going to improve the garbage collector. Java currently uses a simple mark-and-sweep garbage collector that will occasionally cause a pause in execution to compact the heap. This is not acceptable for some applications that require real-time performance. Research has shown that it is possible to write pause-free real-time garbage collectors that can greatly reduce the impact of garbage collection.

Yet another reason why Java programs can be more efficient than C programs lies in the multithreading model. It turns out to be very hard to compile a sequential algorithm for a multiprocessor machine and scale the performance linearly with the number of processors. Much research has gone into this, and it looks like it may be better to put the burden on the programmer rather than the compiler. The programmer should be encouraged to introduce lightweight threads into the application. But writing multi-threaded applications in C and C++ is extremely hard (I know because I've tried). There simply isn't much support for multithreading, and there are many pitfalls. The lack of garbage collection makes memory management hard and it is easy to forget to unlock a monitor when returning from a function, or when an exception is thrown.

Java eliminates a lot of these problems, and although it is still possible to cause deadlock, writing a multithreaded application is easy. A Java application that uses fine-grained multithreading will run very efficiently on a multiprocessor machine. Although the current release still uses a home-grown threads package, we have implementations that use native Solaris threads.

CONCLUSION

Java in its current form is only the first step towards creating a better technology framework for Internet applications. There is still much work to do and much to learn. Java is to the Internet what DOS was for personal computers. It is a gigantic step forward, but to become really popular it needs to become the equivalent of Windows 95 (actually, I hope it will be better). This year will be a very exciting one. Java presents an incredible opportunity for emerging small companies. It has leveled the playing field and the software giants no longer have the upper hand. Anyone can start hacking in Java and distribute their products over the Internet in an ever-growing market that soon will be populated with millions of consumers.

The ever-growing Internet, the increasing need for interactivity, the introduction of Internet access devices, and the increasing number of consumers clearly present a great opportunity for Java. There still is much low-hanging fruit when it comes to improving the Java technology. Increased performance, new tools, and increased functionality will keep the developer community interested in the near future.

Java will take the Internet to the next level: the consumer market. This will mean that Internet software has got to become simpler, easier to use, longer lasting, less technology-focused, and more fun. Although Java doesn't provide all the answers for the problems that we are facing, it certainly plays a central role in solving many of them.

Arthur van Hoff was a Senior Staff Engineer at Sun Microsystems. He was with Sun for three years and was involved in the development of Java since 1993. He was the author of the Java compiler, and was the HotJava project lead. He has since left Sun to form a Java start-up company and can be reached by email at avh@netcom.com.

Assessing the Java Security Layers

Joel Scotkin

IN MANY WAYS, Java is a language written in hindsight. The developers were able to design the language with its context in mind. Thus, Java is really the first language constructed in the world of the networked computing environment, and has features and accommodations which are simply not present in other environments. Some of these are obvious—network downloading of classes, for instance. Some of them are more subtle. One of the most important of these features, and a key to Java's success in the business community, is the set of security protections offered by the Java language, the virtual machine, and the class libraries.

There are several types of security that apply to applications built in Java. I will address the impacts and benefits offered by the various Java security layers. The first is safeguard protection, or the set of guarantees offered to the user that aim to protect against malicious code. The second is the more traditional transaction security, which is aimed at securing communications the user might have with remote machines (very important in the new distributed world!). The inclusion of these technologies in the Java environment really opens up the potential of business applications. I would therefore like to begin by taking a fairly close look at the first type of security, which protects users running Java code. Then we'll take a look at how transactional security is expanding the scope of protections offered to users, and how the trust offered by secure transactions can offer real protections to business users.

PLAYING IN THE SANDBOX

Java takes a while to sink in. Early on, I remember bringing up Sun's Java demo page for various people, and showing off the half-dozen or so early

12 INTRODUCTION TO JAVA

examples (spinning heads, bouncing text, real-time spreadsheet). Depending on the audience, the reaction was almost always the same. First, either a lack of comprehension ("This is new? OK."), or a mildly interested grunt of approval. The reason was clear—when I showed off the first demo on the list, people immediately assumed that browsers could now make text move, or heads spin. However, as the demos progressed, everyone suddenly saw a particular screen which jumped out at them, one which finally drove the point home—this was something new. Whether it was the animation or the spreadsheet, the bouncy text or the simulations, it finally dawned that what I was demonstrating was merely the byproduct or subset of what must be a far more powerful tool.

Soon after that the questions would become less about particular demonstrations, and more about potential. As the potential for this brave new world sank in, so did all of the usual (and justified) fears of the unknown. In the business world where I was giving these demos, this soon translated into a single question—can this new flexibility be abused?

This is a very fair question. When browsers were simply tools for displaying text and pictures, there was very little that could go wrong. At most, they would crash, occasionally taking unprotected operating systems down with them. As functionality was added, however, legitimate fears of viruses, rogue applications, and data thieves rose to the forefront. Networks are a two-way street—the possibility that a program that you invited in would siphon all of your data out to someone else, along with all of your passwords, was very real.

Fortunately, raising the question gave people a chance to hear the answer, and the answer was a good one. Sun had put an incredible amount of effort into designing this new environment so that it could completely safeguard the user from rogue applications. There would be no viruses or data snoopers. The Microsoft Word macro virus was a far more dangerous threat. In fact, Java was secure in ways no other language had been secure before, partly as a side effect of the language itself, and partly from some excellent work designing the security for the virtual machine.

Other articles in this issue detail the technical specifications behind the security mechanisms. The basics are fairly simple, however. The most important concept behind the Java run-time security is often called the sandbox. Java applets run in their own protected little area, and by default, are not allowed any access to system resources, including disk access, memory, networking, hardware, etc.

The first part of the sandbox is the language itself. The fact that Java does not offer any direct access to memory offers a strong first barrier to attack. With no direct access to memory, system calls, or system hardware, it is almost impossible to interfere with another running program, or to learn secrets (such as passwords) from the operating system.

The second part of the security is the Java virtual machine. The reason that Java is so portable is that it is essentially compiled for a non-existent but well defined CPU, and then each machine that wants to run Java programs runs a CPU emulator, much the same way a PowerMac can run 68040 code. This emulator essentially provides a virtual (or simulated) machine to run your Java code. The Java virtual machine, or VM, was designed so that emulating its instructions could be done very efficiently. From a security standpoint, then, the Java code is not really running on your computer, with all of the privileges that would imply, but is instead running in a carefully controlled environment, which can monitor all actions.

The VM uses a class called the Security Manager to assign permissions to programs. For instance, you might have noticed that Java applications when run standalone can access your local hard drive, but that the same program running in a browser cannot do so. This is because the browser has a security manager that forbids this access. In the future, we'll start to see browsers which allow users to set parameters in the security manager.

To ensure that nobody tries to subvert the virtual machine, a complex set of security checks are in place. The compiler is designed to only generate correct code. However, this would not stop a determined attacker from writing their own compiler, and then generating code which might somehow crash the VM, or change the security permissions. Therefore, the first thing the VM does when it downloads code is to run it through a four-step checking process known as the byte-code verifier. This does what is says—it runs through all of the code downloaded to make sure that it does not violate any of the rules of the Java language or virtual machine. This guarantees that nobody could have generated their own program to break the rules. As the code runs, the virtual machine checks every action against the list of actions permitted by the security manager, and either allows it to go through, or generates a security exception in the running program.

In a way, this is just a logical extension of the protections which exist in various operating systems. Windows 3.1 and the MacOS run themselves

14   INTRODUCTION TO JAVA

and all programs in the same memory space, and this means that one poorly written program can crash other programs or the entire machine. UNIX and Windows NT, on the other hand, give each program their own virtual memory space, and offer only protected paths between programs and to the operating system functions. This doesn't prevent any single program from crashing, but it does ensure that when it does crash, it cannot affect other programs or the operating system. The sandbox takes this further, offering not just protected memory, but protected access to all system functions. The end result is that as a user, you do not need to worry about attacks on your machine from random code you download. The code is (by default, at least) tightly restricted in its capabilities, and has no mechanisms for loosening these restrictions.

A final note here. Several flaws have been found and widely publicized in this aspect of Java security. All of these flaws, however, were implementation errors, and were quickly fixed as the JDK was updated. No known theoretical holes exist in the security implementation, and currently, there are no outstanding implementation holes that I know of. However, each vendor who decides to write their own virtual machine, as Microsoft and others have done, needs to have their version held up to the same scrutiny as Sun's initial VM. Correct implementation of the various pieces of security can be quite tricky, especially as vendors add enhanced features such as faster garbage collectors, and only very careful analysis and time will serve to ferret out some of the subtler bugs.

WHO DO YOU TRUST?

The second aspect of security is securing information. There are four main keys to securing information—authentication, encryption, authorization and non-repudiation. I discussed these briefly in an earlier column, and here I want to bring the them down to just two pieces—authentication and authorization.

Authentication is simple, in concept. You always want to know who you are talking to, because this offers a certain level of trust. I might accept and install a finance program from my bank, for instance, while I might not accept a similar program that arrived unsolicited through the mail. The new 1.1 JDK has classes designed to prove ownership, particularly the digital signature. This allows developers to prove, in a cryptographically strong manner, that they really were the creator of a particular program or piece of a program.

Authorization is the corollary to authentication. Once I know who I am dealing with, I can choose what to let them access. My big beef with ActiveX is that it provides strong authentication with no authorization—access is an all or nothing proposition. Either you trust code, and it can do anything, including wiping your hard drive or stealing your secrets, or you don't, and then you don't run it. The Java Security Manager allows for selective authorization. Browsers by default do not allow code any liberties whatsoever. However, users can (or will soon be able to) choose how to selectively relax these restrictions. Perhaps you might allow some programs to read and write to a particular directory. Or, you might want to give some trusted applets full privileges. This would make sense in many companies, where you are distributing applications internally over an intranet using a Web browser as the enabling transport technology. Thus, you would give all internal applets full privileges, while keeping applets downloaded from the Internet completely restricted.

The new 1.1 JDK offers this combination of authentication and authorization (but it looks like full transactional security will still have to wait for the next release). This does work to solve many of the current problems with using Java in the corporate environment, such as saving files locally, accessing arbitrary machines across the network, and using advanced features of the native operating system. However, this new freedom comes at a price—configuration vigilance. It will become very important to ensure that desktops are correctly configured with regards to trust and permissions, because a mistake could open access to the wild things waiting in the wings.

SECTION TWO

LANGUAGE FEATURES

Multitasking in Java

Barry Boone

IN JAVA, IMPLEMENTING multitasking is not an operating system hack. It's part of the language and class packages. This is what happens: There is a class called Thread that runs as a lightweight process. To coordinate among different threads, you can use locks. One lock is associated with an object, and one lock associated with its class. If you call an instance method that you've indicated can be executed only by one thread at a time, the called object's lock is used to block access to that method until that method exits (and so automatically releases the lock). The class lock is used with static methods.

You can get multiple threads to weave all through your system simply by instantiating the Thread class or derived classes and starting these instances on their merry ways. Keywords that you specify help Java figure out when and how to coordinate among threads.

THREADS

You can create a new Thread object just as you would any other object:

```
Thread t = new Thread();
```

To start the thread, call its start() method.

```
t.start();
```

This call creates the system resources required to run a new thread and makes Java call the thread's run() method. The thread will live as long as the run() method does not exit and as long as no one calls stop() on the thread.

20   LANGUAGE FEATURES

When the thread does stop, its stop() method gets called. You can subclass and override any of these three methods to perform your own initialization, run instructions, and clean up. At a minimum, you must override run() or your thread won't have any real purpose in life.

Listing 1 gives an example of a simple thread. All this Thread subclass does is override its run() method to show you it is indeed working.

The output from this program is simply:

running...

Let's look at a more involved example of this by checking out what occurs in a town hall meeting. First the emcee gets up and says hello. Then, any speakers that have comments can step up to the podium and give them. The town hall meeting is run in such a way that everyone speaks their mind and no utterance gets lost in the rush to make a case. The emcee allows statements to be heard one at a time. After everyone has said their piece and no other speakers are waiting to say something, the emcee says goodnight, the good citizens leave, and the town hall closes.

We have a number of actors in this play: an emcee and some speakers. Since each of these participants is an individual, we can model each as an individual thread. (However, we will need to provide coordination among them; we'll get to that shortly.)

Listing 1.

```java
class MyClass {
    public static void main(String args[]) {
        MyThread t = new MyThread();
        t.start();
    }
}

class MyThread extends Thread {
    public void run() {
        System.out.println("running...");
    }
}
```

Here's how we can begin to define the participants:

```java
class Speaker extends Thread {
    int        id;
    int        speech_count;
    SynchronizedQueue my_soapbox;

    Speaker(int new_id, int turns,
      SynchronizedQueue forum) {
    id = new_id;
    speech_count = turns;
    my_soapbox = forum;
  }
}

class MC extends Thread {
   SynchronizedQueue podium;

   MC(SynchronizedQueue new_forum) {
      podium = new_forum;
   }
}
```

Speakers wear a name tag (an id). They also arrive with a certain number of points to make (a speech_count). They know where they're going to deliver their wisdom (on my_soapbox). The emcee only needs to know where the podium is. We've also referred to a new class, Synchronized-Queue (which is explained momentarily).

Let's create five speakers at this town hall meeting. We'll enlist the help of a famous political pundit/moderator to assist with our little gathering and assign him the role of emcee:

```java
int num_speakers = 5;

Speaker[] contenders =
 new Speaker[num_speakers];
MC georgeWill = new MC(podium);

georgeWill.start();

for(int i = 0; i < num_speakers; i++) {
   contenders[i] = new Speaker(i, 10, podium);
   contenders[i].start();
}
```

22 Language Features

Notice that for each new Thread we create, we must initiate its start() method. Until we do, it won't actually be doing anything. The Thread instance will exist in memory, but no system resources will be allocated to it to allow it to run as a separate process.

Now let's deal with SynchronizedQueue. The podium will be a subclass we'll create that is a kind of magical and very fair podium: When a speaker says something, the podium will ensure that the speaker's message does not overlay someone else's message and squash that person's equally precious two cents. How this occurs will be described in a few more pages.

Here's the outline for our podium subclass:

```
class SynchronizedQueue extends Vector {

        private int         count;
        private boolean     started;

        SynchronizedQueue() {
        count = 0;
        started = false;
    }
}
```

As you can see from the class definition, the podium knows how many messages are waiting to be said and whether people have started speaking yet.

So what gets said? At this town hall, the citizens are up in arms. There are quite a number of issues on their minds, and they don't hesitate to say them! These issues range from banning monkeys to selling computers, from importing books to outlawing bicycles. A sample town hall session is given in Listing 2.

Why do the good citizens say such things? Well, they only know what they read in the local paper, and everything they read is sorted into nouns and actions and gets stored in their minds. Here's what the speakers' warehouse of activist thoughts looks like:

```
static String nouns[] = {
    "dogs", "cats", "elephants", "donkeys", "houses", "monkeys", "cars",
        "bicycles", "computers", "music", "books" };

static String ends[] = {
    "outlawed", "banned", "imported", "discouraged", "sold", "bought", "given
        away", "made mandatory", "encouraged", "deported", "exported" };
```

Listing 2.

```
MC here: good morning.
speaker 4 stepping onto soapbox
speaker 1 stepping onto soapbox
speaker 3 stepping onto soapbox
speaker 0 stepping onto soapbox
speaker 0: music should be bought
speaker 2 stepping onto soapbox
speaker 1: bicycles should be given away
speaker 3: bicycles should be given away
speaker 4: music should be bought
speaker 2: bicycles should be given away
speaker 1: cars should be bought
speaker 2: cars should be bought
speaker 1: dogs should be exported
speaker 1: elephants should be outlawed
speaker 0: dogs should be banned
speaker 0: music should be deported
speaker 3: cars should be bought
speaker 3: dogs should be exported
speaker 3: elephants should be outlawed
speaker 0: monkeys should be imported
speaker 0: donkeys should be sold
speaker 0: books should be made mandatory
speaker 0: music should be made mandatory
speaker 0: bicycles should be encouraged
speaker 4: dogs should be banned
speaker 4: music should be deported
speaker 3: cars should be given away
speaker 3: cars should be made mandatory
speaker 2: dogs should be exported
speaker 1: cars should be given away
speaker 0: dogs should be given away
speaker 4: monkeys should be imported
speaker 1: cars should be made mandatory
speaker 4: donkeys should be sold
speaker 2: elephants should be outlawed
speaker 2: cars should be given away
speaker 4: books should be made mandatory
speaker 3: houses should be given away
speaker 1: houses should be given away
speaker 1: books should be imported
speaker 0: donkeys should be discouraged
speaker 1: music should be made mandatory
speaker 1: dogs should be made mandatory
speaker 1 stepping off soapbox
speaker 2: cars should be made mandatory
speaker 3: books should be imported
speaker 4: music should be made mandatory
speaker 0 stepping off soapbox
speaker 4: bicycles should be encouraged
speaker 4: dogs should be given away
speaker 3: music should be made mandatory
speaker 2: houses should be given away
speaker 2: books should be imported
speaker 4: donkeys should be discouraged
speaker 4 stepping off soapbox
speaker 3: dogs should be made mandatory
speaker 3 stepping off soapbox
speaker 2: music should be made mandatory
speaker 2: dogs should be made mandatory
speaker 2 stepping off soapbox
MC here: good night.
Town Hall closing.
```

24   Language Features

When speakers say something, they randomly connect a noun to an action. This activity occurs as follows:

```
public void run() {
    int i;
    Random r = new Random();
    my_soapbox.checkIn();
    my_soapbox.enqueue(
        "speaker "+ id +" stepping onto soapbox");

    for (i = 0; i < speech_count; i++) {
        my_soapbox.enqueue("speaker "+ id +":
        " + nouns[Math.abs(r.nextInt())
        %nouns.length] + " should be " + ends
        [Math.abs(r.nextInt())%ends.length]);
    }
    my_soapbox.enqueue("speaker "+ id +" stepping off soapbox");
    my_soapbox.checkOut();
}
```

That is, a speaker checks in at the town hall, steps up to the soapbox, randomly holds forth on what it has read about, and then steps off the soapbox and checks out. The speakers' utterances are not heard by the audience right away. The emcee, as you'll see, helps ensure their statements are heard one at a time.

THE LIFE CYCLE OF A THREAD

Threads have definite life cycles. Depending on where a thread is in its life cycle, it can be in one of a number of states:

- *New thread:* When you create a new thread object, it's raring to go, but until you call its start() method, it's just a new thread without a life.
- *Runnable:* Once you call start(), the thread executes its start() method and calls run(). If someone calls stop() on the thread, or if the run() method exits, the thread will transition to dead. Otherwise, the thread will remain runnable, even if it's not the highest priority thread and so is not actually currently running. A thread can, however, drop out of the runnable state and become not runnable.
- *Not runnable:* A thread can become runnable again, but it can also

MULTITASKING IN JAVA 25

be killed while in this state if someone calls the thread's stop()
method.

- *Dead:* Once a thread dies, it's just waiting to be garbage-collected
  and can't be resuscitated.

A thread can transition in and out of the runnable state during its life in
a number of ways.

Someone can call the thread's suspend() method. If this occurs, the
thread will be restarted only if someone calls its resume() method at some
later time.

Someone can halt the thread for a specified number of milliseconds
using its sleep() method.

The thread will start up again automatically (if its priority is the highest) after the specified number of milliseconds have elapsed.

The thread itself calls wait(). To get a waiting thread going again, you
can use the method notify() or notifyAll(). This wakes up the thread.

The thread could be blocked by another thread hogging I/O. If a
thread B were trying to read from the keyboard at the same time the user
is typing in some data in response to thread A, thread B would just have
to wait. Once the I/O was free again, thread B would continue on. (To
be safer, you can also wrap your I/O in a synchronized method.)

For the town hall, the emcee allows utterances to be heard by taking
them from the podium one at a time. To do this, the podium's dequeue()
method is invoked. Once all the utterances have been heard by the audience, the emcee says good night. At that point, the emcee's thread comes
to an end. Here's what the run() method for the emcee looks like:

```java
public void run() {
   Object utterance;

   System.out.println(
    "MC here: good morning.");

   utterance = podium.dequeue();
   while (utterance != null) {
      System.out.println(utterance);
      utterance = podium.dequeue();
   }

   System.out.println("MC here: good night.");
}
```

26   LANGUAGE FEATURES

So how does the podium dequeue the statements when the emcee retrieves them? First, the podium makes sure there are speakers left. If there are, but there is currently nothing to be said, the podium waits:

```
while (anyoneLeft() && (super.elementCount == 0)) {
    try {
        wait();
    } catch (InterruptedException x) { }
}
```

Here, the thread goes to sleep when it calls wait(). Every time it's awakened, it checks to see if the conditions that put it to sleep have changed. As you have just learned, when a thread calls wait(), the only way it can continue on is to get notified that something has changed. In particular, the thread should be notified either when a speaker checks out or a speaker says something.

If a speaker checks out, there might not be any speakers left, so we might not have anything more to wait for. If a speaker says something, then we can dequeue that utterance and pass it back to the emcee to be heard. So, SynchronizedQueue makes sure it issues a notify() in both of these situations:

```
public synchronized void checkOut () {
    count--;
    notify();
}

public synchronized
  void enqueue(Object elt) {
    super.addElement(elt);
    notify();
}
```

Let's take a look at the synchronized keyword next.

SYNCHRONIZATION AND MONITORS

Here's an example of why it might be bad not to synchronize in the town hall application. The application adds an utterance to the queue by calling the queue's addElement() method.

```
super.addElement(elt);
```

MULTITASKING IN JAVA   27

We, as the consumers of this class package, do not know how the method addElement() is implemented. It might, for example, be implemented as five separate operations:

1. Fetch the queue.
2. Create a new queue that is one element longer.
3. Copy the elements from the old queue to the new queue.
4. Add the new element to the new queue.
5. Replace the old queue with the new queue.

Now, certainly, this might not be the most efficient way to go about this, but the point is that calling addElement() is not necessarily one machine instruction. Any number of things could be occurring within this call.

What would happen if speaker 1 added an element, and got as far as step 4 when speaker 2, running as a separate thread, preempts to add an utterance? If speaker 2 makes it through all 5 steps before speaker 1 is allowed to continue, speaker 1 will overwrite the queue with its own copy and speaker 2's utterance will never be heard by the audience.

To stop speaker 2's comments from becoming lost in the sands of time, we can indicate that only one speaker can add their comments to the queue at any one time. You indicate this by declaring the method to be synchronized.

```
public synchronized void enqueue(Object elt) {
```

How does Java perform this synchronization? Java associates a monitor with each object and with each class. When a thread enters a synchronized method, that thread enters the appropriate monitor as well. When the thread exits the synchronized method, it also exits the monitor. In the preceding example, Java uses the monitor associated with the instance since this is an instance method. If this were a static method, Java would use the monitor associated with the class.

Once you call a synchronized method, any other call to a synchronized method for that instance must wait until the thread exits the monitor. The important concept to grasp here is that Java is performing this synchronization as part of the language. Java is handling all the bookkeeping; all you have to do is use the correct keyword.

Note that a thread exits the monitor for a synchronized method when it calls wait(), as in the example given earlier. Exiting the monitor gives other threads a chance to change the conditions the first thread is waiting on.

AVOIDING DEADLOCK

One tricky logic problem that Java can't always help you avoid is deadlock. It sounds painful, and it is. Specifically, deadlock occurs if more than one thread is running, and each is attempting to access a locked resource guarded by the other.

For example, imagine if the town hall application were implemented a different way. What if a speaker would only say something if that person could step up to an empty podium, and what if the emcee was on the podium waiting for a speaker to step up before the emcee stepped off? Figure 1 portrays the situation.

Java does try to eliminate deadlock situations it can detect. For example, what happens if you implement a recursive algorithm for a synchronized method? Consider Listing 3.

What's the result of Listing 3? Do we hit a deadlock condition, because we lock the instance's monitor with the first call to calculate, and then wait forever in the recursive call to calculate(number - 1), because we're still inside calculate()?

Amazingly, no. Java knows enough to allow the reentry to occur. The secret is that once a thread obtains the lock, it does not have to obtain it again, so recursion is possible for synchronized methods. This program will work just fine.

To help avoid deadlock situations, you should try not to execute one synchronized method from within another synchronized method. If you can do this, you'll never run into trouble. But if this can't be helped, you should at least try to only use a monitor for the shortest amount of time. In particular, try not to lock a method that does something that might take a long time, such as performing a lengthy calculation, writing data to a printer, or accessing files over a network.

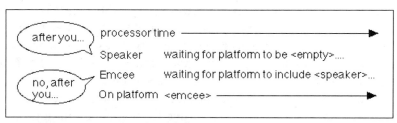

Figure 1. Deadlock with polite town hall participants.

MULTITASKING IN JAVA   29

Listing 3.

```java
class Factorial {
    static public void main(String[] args) {
        Factorial f = new Factorial();
        int result = f.calculate(10);
    }
    synchronized int calculate(int number) {
        if (number == 1)
            return 1;
        else
            return calculate(number - 1) * number;
    }
}
```

To help cut down the amount of time you need to create a lock, you can also lock particular blocks of code rather than entire methods. For that, you use the synchronized statement. You specify the lock you'd like to use in this statement, which can be either a particular instance or a class. For example, to use a class's monitor as a lock, use the synchronized statement like this:

```java
synchronized (MyClass) {
    // ... your locked code goes here
}
```

or, to use an instance, supply the instance in this statement:

```java
synchronized (myObject) {
    // ... your locked code goes here
}
```

When the synchronized block exits or wait() is called, the lock is released.

PRIORITIES

With more than one thing happening at once—that is, with more than one thread—how does Java coordinate among threads? Java uses a fixed priority scheduling algorithm. That is, threads are scheduled based on their priorities. The highest priority thread is always the one that's running. If there's more than one thread with the same highest priority, Java

30 LANGUAGE FEATURES

has the ability to switch between them. Java can perform preemptive multitasking. In particular, the highest priority thread will always be the one that runs. For example, if a lower-priority thread suddenly becomes a higher-priority thread, the other thread will be suspended and the new, higher-priority thread will start executing immediately.

A thread can also yield to other threads that have the same priority as itself (or to new or existing threads that have taken on a higher priority). If a system does not allow preemptive multitasking, yielding control is the only way to get concurrency to happen.

When a thread is created, it takes its priority from the thread that created it. This way, threads run concurrently, with the scheduler switching back and forth between them. You can also explicitly set a thread's priority higher or lower, as long as it falls between the range MIN_PRIORITY and MAX_PRIORITY—values that the Thread class maintains. The default priority is set midway between these two values.

ADVANCED SYNCHRONIZATION

In addition to ensuring only one chunk of code can be accessed at once, you can also synchronize by splicing processes back together.

For example, here's pseudocode for the TownHall class's main() method:

```
create the MC
create the speakers
join the MC's thread with the thread that initiated it
close the town hall
```

What would happen if we did not attempt to join up the MC's thread with the thread that initiated it (which is the thread that's running the main() method)? The town hall would close while the emcee and the speakers were all still inside hashing out the issues! In other words, we'd get output that looked something like this:

```
MC here: good morning.
speaker 4 stepping onto soapbox
speaker 1 stepping onto soapbox
speaker 3 stepping onto soapbox
speaker 0 stepping onto soapbox
speaker 0: music should be bought
speaker 2 stepping onto soapbox
Town Hall closing.
```

speaker 2: dogs should be made mandatory
speaker 2 stepping off soapbox

.

.

.

To join a thread with the thread that initiated it, you simply call the thread's join() method. The emcee for the town hall meeting does this as follows:

```
public static void main(String args[]) {

    // ... create the speakers ...

    MC georgeWill = new MC(podium);
    georgeWill.start();

    // ... let the speakers speak ...

    try {
    georgeWill.join();
    } catch (InterruptedException x) { }

    System.out.println(
        "Town Hall closing.");
}
```

Since we're waiting for the MC thread to come to completion, we have to be prepared to handle an exception if it gets interrupted.

IMPLEMENTING RUNNABLE

Threads can either respond to process method calls directly—in particular, run()—or they can transfer their control to a proxy. To do this, the proxy makes itself the thread's target and indicates it will implement the interface defined by Runnable:

```
class MyApplet extends Applet implements Runnable {

    // ... various applet methods

    public void myMethod() {
        Thread t = new Thread();
        t.target = this;
```

32 LANGUAGE FEATURES

```java
        t.start();
    }
    public void run() {
        System.out.println(
          "the applet is handling run...");
    }

}
```

For example, let's look at a pendulum class, which is discussed in detail in the new book *Java Essentials for C and C++ Programmers.* So that the process that governs the pendulum's swing is running as a separate thread from anything else the application is doing, you can create a class called Pendulum that implements the Runnable interface. You can then create the thread, supplying an instance of your Pendulum class as the thread's target when you invoke the threads constructor, as follows:

```java
public class Pendulum implements Runnable {
        Thread myThread;

    public void startPendulum() {
        if (myThread == null) {
            myThread = new Thread(
              this, "Pendulum");
            myThread.start();
    }
```

When your thread goes to do its thing, it will look to your Pendulum class for its instructions. You can supply them like this:

```java
/** Keep on swinging and redrawing the pendulum. */
public void run() {
    while (myThread != null) {
        swing();
        repaint();
    }
}
```

Barry Boone is the author of *Java Essentials for C and C++ Programmers* and can be reached at barryb@bluehorse.com. Excerpted by permission of Addison-Wesley Publishing from *Java Essentials for C and C+= Programmers* by Barry Boone. (ISBN 0-201-479) ©1996 Barry Boone. To order, call 1.800.822.6339.

Design and Modeling Opportunities in Java

Desmond D'Souza

SO, WHAT'S WITH THE Java buzz, anyway? Anyone who ventures into cyberspace for the first time is invariably somewhat awed by the magnitude and implications of what is happening out there. While the Web transformed the face of the Internet in the early 1990s and linked together its vast resources in an easily accessible way, today Java is poised to take the Web a significant step forward into the world of fully inter-active Web applications, and into the world of distributed objects. However, Java is poised to be much more than an Internet programming language: it is an elegant, consistent, and surprisingly effective general-purpose object-oriented programming language as well, suited to both conventional as well as concurrent and distributed applications. In fact, if I might venture out on a limb with a prediction here—Java is shaping up to become a very serious contender for implementing component-ware, including Micro-soft's COM/ActiveX, OpenDoc, and Corba-based systems, general distributed systems, Web applets, as well as more traditional applications.

In my series of columns on Modelling and Design with Java* in the *Journal of Object Oriented Programming,* I examine Java and related technologies from a variety of perspectives, including design, specifications and models, concurrency, the Web, distributed objects, databases, and ActiveX. In short, this is not going to be a purely programming language article.

---

* This is an edited version of "Java: Design and Modeling Opportunities," which appeared in *JOOP* 9(5), September, 1996.

34 LANGUAGE FEATURES

Here, we examine a specific Java language feature: the interface. Specifically, we will discuss what interfaces represent, and the opportunity they present for design and modeling to define behavioral types. We will then discuss in more detail the relationship between class and interface, and introduce the notion of refinement for effectively describing this relationship. Lastly, we will discuss the limitations of refinement based solely on subtyping, and introduce a very expressive form of refinement based on the notion of collaborations adapted from the Catalysis method (*Catalysis: Practical Rigor and Refinement,* Prentice Hall, forthcoming).

THE JAVA "INTERFACE"

One of the most serious errors made in many common object-oriented languages is the failure to distinguish type from class, i.e., interface versus implementation. The same, unfortunately, was true of some leading methodologies. Perhaps the implementation language constructs in Java will help improve popular analysis and modeling methods and languages.

C++: Subclasses inherit both implementation and interface. While it is possible to inherit implementation without interface by hiding the interface behind private inheritance, it is not possible to do the opposite: conform to an interface without using its implementation. The compiler only permits substitution of objects known at compile time to be instances of a class derived (interface + implementation) from another.

Smalltalk: Subclasses inherit implementation from superclasses. Each class can support multiple protocols independently of the inheritance structure. The language only checks at runtime to ensure that the interface required by a client is actually object-supported, by looking up each message send dynamically. Some programmers informally use the protocol facility to organize interfaces.

Objective-C: Subclasses inherit interface and implementation from superclass. There is, in addition, an explicit facility for protocols, very analogous to Java's interface.

Eiffel: Despite supporting semantic specification of classes by pre/post-conditions and invariants, Eiffel also fails to make the distinction between type and class.

The Java interface (*The Java Language Reference Manual, Sun Microsystems,* 1996) is used to define the interface a client can expect from an object, regardless of what class and superclass structure is used to implement that object. Any number of classes can independently provide implementations for an interface.

```
interface List {
    void addItem (Item toAdd);
    void addItem (Item toAdd, int position);
    Item delItem (int position);
}
```

Classes define implementations and provide interfaces.

```
class LinkedList implements List {
    public void addItem (Item toAdd);
    public void addItem (Item toAdd, int position) { ...... }
    public Item delItem (int position) { ...... }
        private List_Node first;
}
```

Any number of classes can implement the same interface, and a class can implement any number of interfaces. For example, suppose we had another interface Selector, which provided the ability to select a single item at a time (e.g., for a mouse-clickable list-box).

```
interface Selector {
    void select (Item toSelect);
    void deSelect (Item toDeselect);
    void activate (Item toActivate);
    Item getSelectedItem();
}
```

We can then have a class which provided two interfaces (see Fig. 1), one to the user through the GUI, the other to the application or problem-domain objects.

```
class ListBox implements Selector, List {
    // ——- Selector operations
    public void select (Item toSelect) { ....... }
    public void deSelect (Item toDeselect) { ....... }
    public void activate (Item toActivate) { ...... }
    public Item getSelectedItem() { ..... }
    // ——- List operations
    public void addItem (Item toAdd) { ..... }
    public void addItem (Item toAdd, int position) { ....... }
```

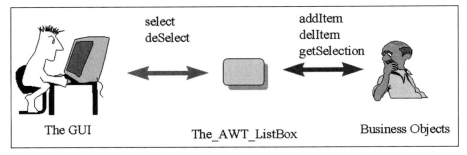

Figure 1.

```
    public Item delItem (int position) { ....... }
    // ——- private implementation
    private .....
}
```

A client should, at all times, only be aware of the interface of the objects it deals with, not their class. The only place where client code needs to name a class is when instantiating a new object. Even in that situation, careful design using factory-like design patterns will alleviate the dependencies a lot.

CLIENT'S VIEW: INTERFACES AS BEHAVIORS

An interface is very much a pure "type" i.e., it describes no more than what a client needs to know. Of course, simply looking at the signatures of a set of methods does not tell the client what those methods will do, and how they should be used (see Fig. 2). For example, where do items get added by default? How is position defined? Clearly, any valid implementation must conform to certain behavioral guarantees. The interface signatures themselves do not describe these behavioral guarantees.

If we try to describe the operations, we will find ourselves relying on an *underlying vocabulary*. For example:

    addItem (i, p) spec { the item i has been added at position p and is selected }

this immediately uncovers more questions and further underlying vocabulary: What are valid values for i, p? What about the previous item which was at position p? Proceeding along these lines, we try to find a common vocabulary that relates all the operations on this interface:

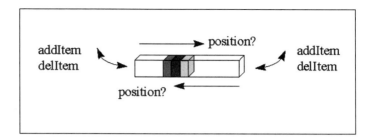

Figure 2.

- addItem (item, pos)
- pos must be between 1 and *current count* + 1
- the item i *has been inserted* at position and is now selected
- all previous items from pos to current count *moved up* by 1
- delItem (pos)
- pos must be between 1 and *current count*
- the *previous item* at pos has been returned
- all previous items from pos+1 to current count *moved down* by 1

Clearly, this vocabulary has to be a part of the interface. It is not too useful to agree to a syntactic interface unless we also agree to the common vocabulary and behavior required of that interface, so that two different clients have the same understanding and expectation as an implementor of that interface.

Figure 3.

38 LANGUAGE FEATURES

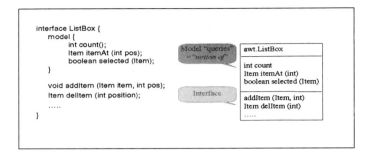

Figure 4.

We make these guarantees explicit by introducing a *model* for that interface. A model is a set of *hypothesized queries* that are used to define required behavior. This model has to be understood by a client, even if no functions actually implement them (they do not have to be invocable at runtime—hence the term hypothesized queries). Taking a small liberty with Java syntax, we introduce this model as a part of the definition of the interface, with a visual modeling and design notation (see Fig. 4). Please note that the model is not an implementation.

This model is not an end in itself. The primary reason for building this model is to allow us to specify behaviors (see *Behavior-driven vs. Data-driven Methodologies: A Non-Issue*, http://www.iconcomp.com/papers). We can now define the behavior of our Listbox as a test which any correct implementation should satisfy, in terms of how those queries change as the result of an operation, and how any output values (or messages) relate to those queries (see Fig. 5). This contract is specified using the form: spec { preconditions :- postconditions }. Note that movedUp is an auxiliary model query; it has been introduced as a convenient way to defer a detailed description of moving items up.

Interfaces described with a clear model ("vocabulary") and behaviors are far easier to use than plain signature sets. But what is wrong with signature sets complemented with, say, comment blocks? Informal textual documentation of an interface should never go away. However, as soon as the vocabulary and operations start to become nontrivial, it becomes critical to have a more rigorous basis for the narrative. If not, the descriptions very quickly end up being inconsistent and ambiguous.

IMPLEMENTORS VIEW: THE "HOW"

If I provide my own implementation of this interface, how do I make use of the behaviors specified in the interface? An implementation can

Design and Modeling Opportunities in Java   39

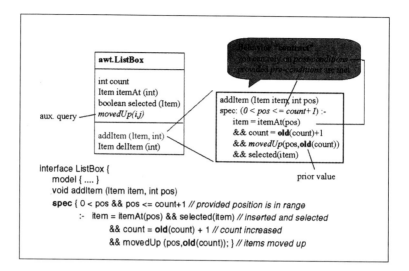

Figure 5.

choose any representation it needs, and can implement operations against that representation. However, any valid implementation must support the abstract vocabulary defined by the model in the interface. Thus, every model query should be definable (i.e., mapped to) in terms of the actual representation chosen. The implemented operation should then map to the behavior specified in the interface.

Here we implement our interface using two data members:

```
class ListBoxA implements ListBox {
    // ---- Private data
    List items;
    Item selection;

    // ---- ListBox operations
    addItem (Item toAdd, int position) {
        items.insertAt (item, position);
        selection = item;
    }
}
```

Our implementation must map to the queries defined in the interface. Such a mapping is called a retrieval, as it "retrieves" the abstract concepts (in this case, queries) from a specific implementation of those concepts (in this case, the selected data representation). Figure 6 illustrates the *implements* relation, and how the corresponding retrieval might be presented in a tool (together with narrative text, as always).

40 Language Features

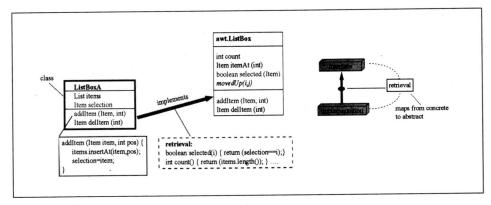

Figure 6.

This approach to relating interfaces to implementations via a retrieval is very attractive because it combines:

1. Precise statement of behavior in terms of an abstract model
2. No unnecessary constraints on alternative implementations of that behavior

Terminology and Summary

Here are some definitions from Catalysis which apply to our discussion:

Type: A (specification of a) set of objects (implemented through any mechanisms, including classes, sub-classes, etc.) that exhibit a common behavior (as described in the specification of that type).

Type-model: A hypothesized set of *queries* that define an abstract view of state (and, in advanced usage, state changes) of all objects of that type.

Refinement: A relationship between abstract and concrete descriptions. The term also defines how the abstract view is provided by the concrete model, using a *retrieval*. When a class implements an interface, we are applying one kind of refinement with a corresponding retrieval. The Catalysis method is based on a powerful set of refinements.

Desmond D'Souza is President and Chief Scientist of ICON Computing in Austin, TX. He may be reached at dsouza@suez.iconcomp.com.

Java Goes International

Rex Jaeschke

IN RECENT YEARS, there has been an increasing interest in, and demand for, serious and standardized support for culture-specific data processing. This is happening particularly within countries having multiple languages and cultures (e.g., Belgium, Canada, and Switzerland). And as national economies become linked, there is a steadily increasing demand for software export. However, users prefer to deal with program interfaces using their own cultural conventions, and rightly so.

An *internationalized program* is one that has no dependency on any culture. The term *internationalization* is often referred to as I18N, because there are 18 letters between the "i" and the "n". For most programs to be useful, they must perform some form of I/O. (Even a seemingly culture-independent program like an operating system has to accept commands and produce messages.) This requirement gives rise to localization (also known as L10N), the process of adapting an internationalized program to a specific cultural environment.

Is Java up to the task of internationalization? After all, access to the World Wide Web, Java's initial area of deployment, is available to anyone on the planet with a PC, modem, an Internet service provider, and a reasonable telephone system. However, before we get into the technical details, let's take a minute to see just how provincial you are and to get you on the right wavelength. Quickly answer the following 5 questions:

1. What happens to the cursor in a text editor when the Enter/Return key is pressed in insert mode?
2. How many lowercase letters are there?
3. It's 11:00 A.M. in New York City. Ignoring differences in Daylight Savings Time, what time is it in Frankfurt, Germany, six time zones to the East?

42 LANGUAGE FEATURES

4. Write the following amount as a number: three thousand four hundred point five.
5. What date does 1/12/10 represent?

Surprise, there are no absolute answers; the correct answer depends on your context. For example, does your native writing system read left-to-right, right-to-left, or down the page? Does your native character set have the same number of upper- and lowercase letters? Does it even have the notion of case? Do you use a 12- or 24-hour clock? How do you write a thousands separator and radix point? Do you put the day before the month or vice versa? Do you use eras instead of centuries? Okay, now that you're a little more cognizant of the problems software internationalization must address, let's get on with some details.

According to the Design Goals set forth in Sun's JDK v1.1 documentation, "Traditionally, internationalization has been a separate process that is optionally performed after normal development. This model does not work for developers writing Internet programs in 'Internet Time.' By contrast, Java programs should be internationalized by default. This implies that it should be easier than not to write internationalized Java code." By and large, with the I18N support provided by v1.1, this goal appears to have been met; however, I'm sure we'll see more extensions and enhancements in this direction in future releases, especially as users gain more experience.

When it comes to I18N, we must deal with two primary issues: *character set representation* and *cultural differences*. Because the two are independent, we'll cover them separately.

CHARACTER SET REPRESENTATION

The designers of Java took the bold step of defining a language whose basic character type could accommodate characters from all the world's current (as well as a few ancient) writing systems; they chose Unicode, a 16-bit character set also known as ISO 10646.UCS-2. (The JDK v1.1 supports v2.0 of the Unicode specification.) For years, language standards committees, implementers, and programmers have been wrestling with various approaches to handling large alphabets. The end result has mostly been a beast called a *multibyte character* that contains one or more bytes, possibly with shift-state encoding. Now that disk and memory capacities are plentiful and cheap and data transmission speed is still on the increase, it's been deemed acceptable to force every character to be 16 bits even though the native alphabets in the western and much of the eastern world need only eight. Of course, such a radical change can only come with a new language; Java just happened to be the agent of change. So a character in Java corresponds to what is commonly known as a wide character in other languages, most notably in C and C++.

The issue of character sets can be broken down into two subcategories: *source character set* and *execution character set*. Let's look at the provisions for expressing source code first.

SOURCE CHARACTER SET

In an ideal world, we'd all throw away our ASCII/EBCDIC-based tools and replace them with those that understand Unicode, and we'd be able to print and display every Unicode character. However, old habits die hard, replacement tools cost money, and there's often a nontrivial psychological obstacle to change—e.g., my tried and proven text editor doesn't understand long filenames so editing a Java or HTML source file is an obstacle, but I'm not looking to upgrade my editor. Heck, I'm still using a perfectly good spell checker that doesn't understand subdirectories (introduced on my system back in 1983!).

In the meantime, Java contains the provision for expressing any source character as a Unicode escape sequence of the form \uhhhh, where hhhh is a 4-digit hexadecimal number signifying the character's internal value. (This approach is equivalent to using trigraphs and digraphs in C/C++.) Because Java permits variable and method names, for example, to be written using any Java letter, we've got problems if we have to maintain source code containing Greek or Russian identifiers using an ASCII-based editor.

And whereas not all Java compilers will accept input in this form, JDK v1.1's javac will. In fact, that implementation goes one step further by providing a more sensible tool called *native2ascii*. This program converts a file with native-encoded characters (characters which are non-Latin 1 and non-Unicode) to one with Unicode-encoded characters and vice versa.

Any Unicode character can be used inside string literals, character constants, and in comments, and any letter can be used in user-defined names. And that nicely addresses the source code issues, at least from a pure Java perspective. However, native methods must deal with Java's

44 LANGUAGE FEATURES

wide characters and development tools often can't deal with exotic external name spellings. So there's work to be done when passing Strings between Java and C/C++ even if only ASCII characters are used; every Java character is simply 16 bits wide.

Whether the source language accepted by your Java compiler is ASCII, EBCDIC, Unicode, or something else, there is a standard and portable way to convert from one format to the other using Unicode escape sequences.

Even though we can embed all kinds of interesting characters inside string literals and character constants, we need a more abstract approach if the same code is to handle multiple languages. Specifically, we must avoid hard-coding such text in the code. One simple way to address this is to create one or more message classes that contain the text. Consider the following example:

```java
import java.io.*;

class MessageString {
    public static void main(String[] args)
    {
        System.out.println(Message.ASK_NAME);
    }
}
```

If we wish to build an English version of this program, we compile the English version of the Message class, which contains the following:

```java
public class Message {
    static final String ASK_NAME = "What is your name?";
}
```

And if we want a Spanish version, we compile the Spanish version of Message:

```java
public class Message {
    static final String ASK_NAME = "Cómo se llama?";
}
```

And, of course, we can create a new version of Message for each language we wish to support. However, this approach permits only one language to be supported at a time. And while that is sufficient for many programs, some programs need to work with multiple languages simultaneously.

This approach also has another limitation. Not all strings need to be printed verbatim; in many cases, we need to insert some values in the string. The trick is to insert them in the correct place. For example, in the following three language versions, in which %1 is a place-holder for some variable's value, how can we substitute the value?

English: There are %1 days in a week.
Spanish: Hay %1 dias en una semana.
German: Es gibt %1 Tage in einer Woche.

Sentence order varies considerably between languages. For example, the English sentence "Among them, the 20 students owned 15 cars." might have the student count come after the car count when written in another language. Therefore, in such a case, the substitution strings must also be inserted in the correct order for each language.

EXECUTION CHARACTER SET

Java's execution set is Unicode and since every Unicode character can be expressed in the source one way or another, each can also be expressed as a Unicode character at runtime.

An important character set issue is one of display. In v1.0, most of the I/O routines that supposedly trafficked in chars, really truncated them to their low-order byte. However, things have improved in v1.1, which introduced character streams. These new streams traffic in 16-bit characters instead of 8-bit bytes and they are built on top of two new classes called Reader and Writer. Basically, they provide an I/O capability that mirrors the existing I/O library. Whereas these classes are built on top of the old byte-oriented family, they contain an intermediate layer that translates from a native (multibyte) encoding to Unicode on input and vice versa on output. The good news here is that the on-disk character encoding is transparent; for example, whether Japanese text is stored using JIS, Shift-JIS, or EUC encoding won't matter to the programmer. PrintStream has also been upgraded to deal with 16-bit characters.

CULTURAL DIFFERENCES

During 1986-1987, the ANSI C committee, in conjunction with I18N experts from various companies, came up with the notion of a locale, a

46 LANGUAGE FEATURES

set of conventions based on some nationality, culture, or language. A locale in C is made up of a set of categories each of which provides support for one distinct part of I18N. These categories are: collating sequence, character classification, monetary formatting, numeric formatting, and time/date formatting. By default, a program would start executing in some default locale and the program could set to an explicit locale by calling a library function. The program could run in a pure or a mixed locale. For example, in a pure locale, such as that used in the U.S. or the U.K., all categories are set to the same target, while in a mixed locale, each category's target can be different. A mixed locale is used in locations in which locale conventions are taken from different cultures, as often happens in towns near borders in Europe.

While Java v1.1 also supports the notion of a locale, the implementation is somewhat different than that provided with C compilers. In particular, C is not an OO-language so its approach doesn't take advantage of Java's OO-capability. Also, the C standard is based on a single-threaded program model, so it ignores the possibility of having thread-specific locales. And C's model does not easily cater to having different objects of the same type have different locale requirements.

JAVA LOCALES

Locale information is encapsulated in an object of type java.util.Locale. When a program begins execution, it has a default locale, which can be retrieved via getDefault(). We can set the default as follows:

```
Locale.setDefault(new Locale("en", "US"));
```

that establishes the language English as spoken in the United States. (Language codes contain two lowercase letters while country codes contain two uppercase letters; both sets of codes conform to ISO standards.) These codes can be obtained from any locale by calling getCountry() and getLanguage().

One of the main problems with locales is which ones will be supported by vendors. Clearly, we cannot mandate that every language/library implementer make every locale in the world available. In the v1.1 specification, the most common Western European and Far East language/country combinations are supported.

We can obtain the textual description of a locale via getDisplay-Name(); for example:

Locale.getDefault().getDisplayName()

which, given a U.S. English default, returns the string "English (United States)." So far, these examples have worked much like those in C: we set a global default and all subsequent locale-specific operations are done in that context. However, we can call methods having locale-specific behavior giving them a locale other than the default. For example:

Locale.getDefault().getDisplayName (Locale.GERMANY)

returns the name of the default locale as it would be written in the german locale; that is, as "Englisch (Vereinigte Staaten)." Note the use of the static final constant GERMANY. The locales corresponding to the most commonly used languages and countries are made available as constants. For example, the constructor used earlier

new Locale("en", "US")

can simply be replaced with

Locale.US

We can create as many locale objects as we wish and we can operate using those locales rather than using the default one; for example,

Locale germany = Locale.GERMANY;

Now if we print out the strings returned from germany.getDisplayLanguage() and germany.get DisplayCountry(), we'll see the locale's language and country names written according to the default locale; that is, as follows:

German Germany

Whereas if they are displayed according to French and German locales, respectively, we would get

allemand Allemagne
Deutsch Deutschland

OTHER SUPPORT

Time and date processing is handled by a number of classes: Calendar, GregorianCalendar, TimeZone, and SimpleTimeZone, all in java.util.

48 LANGUAGE FEATURES

Numbers can be formatted according to local mathematical or currency rules using the classes Format, NumberFormat, and ChoiceFormat, and a host of other classes all part of the new package java.text. MessageFormat is especially useful for dealing with strings that need to have values substituted in them.

Earlier, we showed a way to store text and constants outside the mainstream code by putting them in a target-specific class as static final fields. The package java.util now provides a family of classes to deal with what are called *Resources*. These classes are: ResourceBundle, ListResourceBundle, and PropertyResourceBundle. In the simplest and least flexible approach, we provide different implementations of a series of methods, one implementation per target, and the corresponding target's class is loaded dynamically based on the current locale. The more abstract approach uses property files to store this information.

CONCLUSION

We have barely scratched the surface of the I18N support provided in v1.1. If this discussion has whetted your appetite, your next best move is to download the v1.1 JDK from the JavaSoft Web site, study the documentation, and try it out.

Rex Jaeschke is chair of the ANSI C standards committee that pioneered the idea of locales and provided standardized language support for internationalization in C. He also participates in the pre-standards work of the ISO Java Study Group and teaches seminars on Java, C/C++, Internationalization, and the 32-bit API. He can be reached at +1 703.860.0091 or rex@aussie.com.

URL
JavaSoft
  http://java.sun.com/

SECTION THREE

JAVA VS. C++

Java and C++:
A Critical Comparison

Robert C. Martin

SOFTWARE ENGINEERS ARE being forced to become multilingual. Any of you who have had the pleasure of creating a Web site know this. Reading this article will be something like that. I freely swap C++ and Java throughout.

I want to make it very clear this is not a diatribe against one language or another. I happen to like both Java and C++ quite a bit. I have been a long-time programmer in C++, and have just begun to program in Java. I find programming in Java to be a joy. But then, I find programming in any language to be a joy, even JCL ;-).

This article is simply a discussion of the differences in the two languages. I will not be commenting heavily on deficiencies in C++. These are already very well documented (see Ian Joyner's famous critique of C++. For a copy write to: ian@syacus.acus. oz.au). I will, however, be commenting about both the good and bad points that I perceive in Java. When I have good things to say, this should not be taken as a recommendation of Java. By the same token, when I have bad things to say, this should not be taken as an admonition against the use of Java. In both cases, it is just me venting my opinion. Nothing more.

Up front, I'll say that I am looking forward to writing lots of neat Java applications and applets. But I am not going to give up C++ any time soon either.

This article is a reprint from the January 1997 issue of *C++ Report*, *9*(1), pp. 42–49.

52   JAVA VS. C++

MULTIPLE INHERITANCE

The designers of Java avoided multiple inheritance. Replacing it is multiple conformance to *interfaces*. In Java, there is a structure called an "Interface." A Java interface is almost identical to a C++ class that has nothing but pure virtual functions. In Java, you cannot inherit from more than one base class—even if the base classes have nothing but abstract methods (pure virtual functions). However, you *can* "implement" more than one "interface"—which amounts to the same thing.

For example, in Java you can create the interface for a Stack as follows:

```
public interface Stack
{
    public void Push(Object o);
    public Object Pop();
}
```

This structure is roughly identical to the following C++ code:

```
class Stack
{
    public:
virtual void Push(Object&) = 0;

virtual Object& Pop() = 0;
};
```

However, a Java interface is *not* a class. The functions declared within a Java interface cannot be implemented within that interface. Moreover, a Java interface cannot have any member variables.

Because interfaces cannot have function implementations or data members, multiple implementation of interfaces does not lead to the problems that caused "virtual" inheritance to be added to C++. That is, in Java there is no need for virtual inheritance because it is impossible to inherit the same member variable from more than one path.

In C++, these situations arise from the so-called *deadly diamond of death*. See Figure 1.

This UML 9.1 diagram shows four classes arranged in the diamond structure that creates the need for virtual inheritance. Both of the classes B and C inherit from class A. D multiply inherits from both B and C.

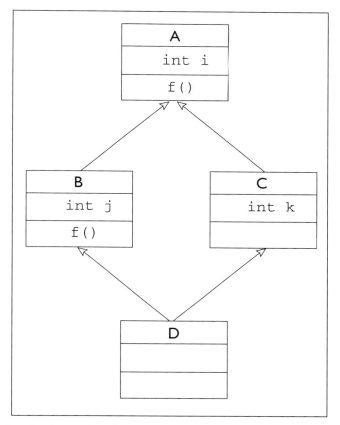

Figure 1. Deadly diamond of death.

Two problems arise from this. First, which implementation of the "f" function does D inherit? Should it inherit B::f() or A::f()? In C++, the answer turns out to be *neither.* D::f() must be declared and implemented. This eliminates the ambiguity and certainly this simple rule could have been adopted in Java.

The second problem, however, is quite a bit more complicated. The class A has a member variable named i. Both classes B and C inherit this member variable. Since D inherits from both B and C, we face an ambiguity. On the one hand, we might want B::i and C::i to be separate variables in D; thus creating two copies of A in D. On the other hand, we might want a single copy of A in D so that only one A::i exists in D.

In C++, we choose between these two options by varying the *kind* of inheritance we use. If we want two copies of A in D, then we use regular

54   Java vs. C++

inheritance from B to A and from C to A. If, however, we want only one copy of A in D, then we use virtual inheritance from B to A and from C to A.

Virtual inheritance is a complex feature and creates problems for compiler implementers and application programmers alike. The designers of Java did not want to have to deal with this issue. So by disallowing multiple inheritance of classes and only allowing the multiple implementation of interfaces, they set the language up such that the *deadly diamond of death* (DDD) cannot lead to ambiguities.

This was probably a good trade-off. In all likelihood it has simplified the language appreciably. However, it has left a problem. It prevents us from inheriting implementation from more than one class in cases where the DDD does not appear. This is unfortunate because it is often the case that we want to inherit from more than one base class which has functions and data.

For example, consider the following C++ program that uses the Observer pattern (Gamma, E., et al, *Design Patterns: Elements of Reusable Object-Oriented Software,* Addison-Wesley, 1995).

```
class Clock
{
   public:
      virtual void Tick() // called once a // second to maintain the time.
      {itsTime++;}
   private:
      Time itsTime;
};
```

We have a Clock class that understands the mathematics of time, and which receives a "Tick" event once per second. We would like to create a version of this class that is *observed.* That is, we want to be able to inform other classes when the state of the Clock class has changed. For this, we use the Observer pattern.

The Observer pattern involves two base classes. One is called Observer; it is an abstract base class with one pure virtual function: Update(). Any class that wants to be informed when the state of an observed class changes must inherit from Observer.

```
class Observer
{
```

Java and C++: A Critical Comparison 55

```
    public:
        virtual void Update() = 0;
};
```

The class that forms the other half of the Observer pattern is named Subject. The Subject class maintains a list of Observer instances and has two concrete functions. The first function, Register, allows instances of Observer to be added to the list. The second function, Notify, is called when there is a state change that needs reporting. This function calls Update on all the registered Observer instances.

```
class Subject
{
    public:
        void Register(Objserver& o)
        {itsObservers.Add(&o);}
        void Notify()
        {
            for (vector<Observer*>::iterator i = itsObservers.begin(); i; i++)
                (*i)->Update();
        }
    private:
        vector<Observer*> itsObservers;
};
```

If you want to create a class that observes state changes in another class, the observing class must inherit from Observer. The observed class must inherit from Subject. The observer class must be registered with the subject class. And the subject class must call Notify when its state is changed.

Back to the clock problem. Not all applications are interested in observing our Clock class; so we don't want to have Clock inheriting from Subject. If we did, then every application would be forced to include the Subject class, even though it didn't need it.

To prevent Subject from existing in every application that uses Clock, we employ multiple inheritance. We create a new class called Observed-Clock that inherits from both Subject and Clock.

```
class ObservedClock : public Clock, public
    Subject
{
    public:
```

56   JAVA VS. C++

```
        virtual void Tick()
        {Clock::Tick(); Notify();}
};
```

This use of multiple inheritance in C++ yields a simple and elegant solution to our problem. Clock is still free to be used in applications that don't need Subject. Those applications that want to observe clock objects can use ObservedClock.

In Java, one cannot do this. Rather one must do the following:

```
public class Clock
{
    public void Tick() {itsTime.Add(1);}
    private Time itsTime;
}

public interface Observer
{
        public void Update();
}

public interface Subject
{
    public void Register(Observer o);
    public void Notify();
}
```

The Clock class is not surprising. The Observer is very similar to the C++ version. In Java, it is an interface, whereas in C++ it was a class with nothing but pure virtual functions. However, the Subject class is quite different. In Java, it too is an interface. But in C++ it was a concrete class with member variables and implemented functions. The implementation of the Subject interface is accomplished in a class named SubjectImpl:

```
public class SubjectImpl implements Subject
{
    public void Register(Observer o)
    {itsObservers.addElement(o);   }

    public void Notify()
    {
        Enumeration i = itsObservers.elements();
```

Java and C++: A Critical Comparison 57

```
    while(i.hasMoreElements())
    {
        Observer o = (Observer)
            (i.nextElement());
        o.Update();
    }
}
private Vector itsObservers;
}
```

We can see that this is very similar to the C++ version. However, Java does not allow multiple inheritance like C++ does, so we have a problem. We cannot inherit from both Clock and SubjectImpl. Instead, we must inherit from Clock and implement the Subject interface. This amounts to multiple inheritance of interface since the ObservedClock class has the union of the Clock and Subject interface:

```
class ObservedClock extends Clock implements Subject
{
    public void Tick() {super.Tick(); Notify();}
    public void Notify() {itsSubjectImpl.Notify();}
    public void Register(Observer o)
        {itsSubjectImpl.Register(o);}
    private SubjectImpl itsSubjectImpl;
}
```

Notice what we had to do. We had to implement the Subject interface by creating a member that points to a SubjectImpl. We then had to delegate every Subject interface to that contained SubjectImpl.

This use of aggregation instead of multiple inheritance is inconvenient to say the least, especially when it must be used with a pattern that is as prevalent as Observer.

This leads me to believe that the Java language will either need a more complete form of multiple inheritance or it will need some new syntax that allows the compiler to automatically delegate. e.g.,

```
class ObservedClock extends Clock delegatesTo SubjectImpl....
```

This proposed delegatesTo syntax would automatically cause Observed-Clock to implement the interface of SubjectImpl as well as automatically forwarding all calls to that interface to an automatically contained instance of SubjectImpl.

58 JAVA VS. C++

MEMORY MANAGEMENT

Java uses garbage collection. Garbage collection is a scheme of memory management that automatically frees blocks of memory sometime after all references to that memory have been redirected. For example, consider the following snippet of Java:

```
Clock c = new Clock(); // c refers to the // new clock.
// ... use c for awhile.
c = null;   // done with that clock.  System will
            // clean up later.
```

In this example, we create a new Clock object using the keyword: new. The new object is referred to by the variable "c". Note that "c" is rather like a reference variable in C++; however, in Java it is possible to reassign references. We use the new Clock object through its reference variable "c" for awhile. Then, when we are done with it, we redirect "c" to null. When the Java runtime system detects that there are no more reference variables referring to the Clock object, it classifies that object as "garbage." At some later time, the Java runtime system will clean up that "garbage," returning its memory to the heap.

Garbage collection makes certain kinds of applications much easier to program. The designers of those programs need not worry as much about cleaning up after "dead" memory. As a result, C++ is often criticized for its lack of GC. However, many people have added garbage collectors to C++. Some of these are available as third party products or as shareware on the net. These collectors are far from perfect, but they can be used when convenient.

The corresponding statement cannot be made for Java. There is *no way* that this humble writer could discover to manage memory manually. Apparently, you cannot write your own memory manager and construct objects within the memory that it controls.

There is a sound reason for this. Any memory management scheme that allows a program to hold pointers or references to unused space allows certain security violations. For example, consider the following program in C++:

```
void f()
{
    char* p = new char[1000000];
```

JAVA AND C++: A CRITICAL COMPARISON   59

```
delete [] p;
SeachForPasswordsInSeparateThread(p);
return;
}
```

The last function called—SearchForPaswordsInSeparateThread—returns immediately. However, it also starts a new thread that continuously scans the megabyte pointed to by p. Because this megabyte has been returned to the heap already, it will be used by lots of other functions in the system. It is just possible that it might be used to hold a password or some other security sensitive material. This material is open to examination by any function that holds a dead pointer into the heap.

Thus, any form of manual memory management that involves holding on to dead pointers or references could result in a security breach. In the typical Java environment, security is a serious concern. Java applets are often downloaded and run in Web browsers. The users may have no idea what applets are running because of their browsing activities. If manual memory management were allowed, it might be possible for unscrupulous people to put up Web pages that contained insecure applets. These applets would be downloaded into the systems of unsuspecting users who happened to browse that page. Once downloaded those applets could then transmit private information back to the author of the Web page.

Is the lack of manual memory management in Java a problem? In most cases, no. However, the lack of manual memory management makes Java a difficult language to use in applications that have hard real-time constraints. The problem is that it is very difficult to predict when the garbage collector will run. When it does run, it can use significant amounts of CPU time. Consider the following Java snippet:

```
public class RealTime
{
    public void Do()    // must complete in 500µs
    {
        Clock c = new Clock;    // might collect!
        // diddle with clock for 100µs
    }
}
```

Here we have a function that must complete in 500 µs. This is a typical constraint in a hard real-time system. Those functions that call RealTime.Do() depend on the fact that it will take no longer than 500 µs to

60 JAVA VS. C++

execute. In many cases, this is a hard constraint that must be met every time Do() is called. However, every once in a while the Java runtime system will be unable to allocate the new Clock object until it has collected garbage and returned unused memory to the heap. There is no telling how long this collection will take. And so, under these circumstances, RealTime.Do() cannot meet its real-time constraints.

One cannot simply follow James Gosling's and Ken Arnold's (*The Java Programming Language,* Addison-Wesley, 1995) advice when they say: "[Garbage Collection] can interfere with time critical applications. You should design systems to be judicious in the number of objects they create." Instead, in time-critical applications, you must design ways in which the memory you need can be made available without the possibility of incurring a garbage collection. One simple strategy is as follows:

```java
public class ClockPool
{
    ClockPool()
    {
        for (int i=0; i<10; i++)
            itsClocks.push(new Clock());
    }
    public Clock GetClock()
    {return (Clock)(itsClocks.pop());}

    public void FreeClock(Clock c) {itsClocks.push(c);}

    private Stack itsClocks;
}
```

Here we have created a simple memory manager. It manages Clock objects. If you need a Clock object you simply call GetClock(). When you are done with it you call FreeClock(). It creates 10 Clock objects for this purpose and holds them in reserve. If more than 10 Clock objects are needed, an exception will be thrown by the Stack when it underflows.

One might think that this solves the problem. Now the RealTime class could be written as follows:

```java
public class RealTime
{
    public void Do(ClockPool p) // must
        // complete in 500µs
```

```
        {
            Clock c = p.GetClock();
            // diddle with clock for 100μs
            p.FreeClock(c);
        }
    }
```

However, we are fiddling with the java.util.Stack class within ClockPool! Is it possible that its activities might force a garbage collection? This train of thought will quickly convince us that using any of the Java standard library within time critical applications can lead to garbage collection.

It should be clear that using Java in hard real-time applications presents some interesting challenges. Caveat Emptor.

FINALIZE

The finalize function in Java roughly corresponds to the destructor in C++. When an object is collected by the garbage collector, its finalize method is called. This allows objects to clean up after themselves. However, it should be noted that in most cases finalize is not a good place to release resources held by the object. It may be a very long time before such objects get collected by the garbage collector. Thus, any resources they release in finalize may be held for a very long time.

Upon normal exit of a Java application, the garbage collector sweeps up all the uncollected objects and their finalize methods are called at that time. (This implies that exiting can take a bit of time). Thus, barring abnormal exits, all finalize methods will eventually be called.

However, there is a convention that one must adopt:

```
class D extends B
{
    protected void finalize() throws
        Throwable
    {
        super.finalize();  // finalize B.
        // now take care of finalizing D.
    }
}
```

62   JAVA VS. C++

The finalize of the derived class must *explicitly* call the finalize of the base class. If you forget to do this, then base class finalize functions simply don't get called. Gosling and Arnold recommend: "Train your fingers so that you always do so in any finalize method you write." *(The Java Programming Language)* Unfortunately, this method is very error prone. In my opinion such "training" belongs to the compiler. The calling of base class finalize methods should have been taken care of by the compiler in the manner of destructors in C++.

TOSTRING()

Any class that has the toString method implemented as follows can be used in some special contexts that expect a String.

```
class MyClass
{
    public String toString()
    {
        return ("MyClass as a String");
    }
}

class Test
{
    public static void main(String[] args)
    {
        MyClass o = new MyClass();
        System.out.println("I just created a Myclass: " + o);
    }
}
```

The use of "o" as an argument of the "+" operator in a String context automatically invokes the MyClass.toString() method. The returned String is then used as the argument of the "+" operator to concatenate the strings. Thus: "I just created a Myclass: Myclass as a String" is printed.

This automatic use of toString() seems to be an immature version of the automatic conversion system of C++. This feature (among others) makes the String class something more special than any other class.

I think it would be wise for the Java designers to work on a generic conversion system. (e.g., a to<xxx> method template)

EXCEPTIONS AND 'FINALLY'

I am very pleased with the exception mechanism in Java. Although modeled after the C++ mechanism, it avoids some of C++'s more severe problems by using the 'finally' clause.

In C++, when an exception leaves the scope of a function, all objects that are allocated on the stack are reclaimed and their destructors are called. Thus, if you want to free a resource or otherwise clean something up when an exception passes by, you must put that code in the destructor of an object that was allocated on the stack. For example:

```
template <class T>
class Deallocator

{
   public:
       Deallocator(T* o) : itsObject(o) {}
       ~Deallocator() {delete itsObject;}
   private:
       T* itsObject;
};

void f() throw (int)
{
   Deallocator<Clock> dc = new Clock;
   // ....things happen, exceptions may be
   // thrown.
}
```

In this example, the Deallocator<Clock> object is responsible for deleting the instance of Clock that was allocated on the heap. Whenever "dc" goes out of scope, either because "f" returns or because an exception is thrown, the destructor for "dc" will be called and the Clock instance will be returned to the heap.

This is artificial, error prone, and inconvenient. Moreover, there are some really nasty issues having to do with throwing exceptions from constructors and destructors that make exceptions in C++ a difficult feature to use well. For more details on the traps and pitfalls of C++ exceptions, I recommend that you read the excellent series of Leading Edge columns by Jack Reeves that have appeared over the past year in *C++ Report*.

64   JAVA VS. C++

Now I am not going to claim that Java has fixed all these things. However, I like their solution better than the C++ solution. Every try block can have a 'finally' clause. Any time such a block is exited, regardless of the reason for that exit (e.g., execution could proceed out of the block or an exception could pass through it), the code in the finally clause is executed.

```
public class Thing
{
    public void Exclusive()
    {
        itsSemphore.Acquire();
        try
        {
            // Code that executes while
            // semaphore is acquired.
            // exceptions may be thrown.
        }
        finally
        {
            itsSemaphore.Release();
        }
    }

    private Semaphore itsSemaphore;
}
```

This Java snippet shows an example of the finally clause. The method Exclusive sets a semaphore and then continues to execute. The finally clause frees the semaphore either when the try block exists or if an exception is thrown.

In many ways, this scheme seems superior to the C++ mechanism. Cleanup code can be directly specified in the finally clause rather than artificially put into some destructor. Also, the cleanup code can be kept in the same scope as the variables being cleaned up. In my opinion, this often makes Java exceptions easier to use than C++ exceptions. The main downside to the Java approach is that it forces the application programmer to (1) know about the release protocol for every resource allocated in a block and to (2) explicitly handle all cleanup operations in the finally block. Nevertheless, I think the C++ community ought to take a good hard look at the Java solution.

THREADS

An in-depth discussion of Java threads is beyond the scope of this article. For more information on Java threads, I recommend that you read Doug Lea's new book (*Concurrent Programming in Java: Design Principles and Patterns,* Addison-Wesley, 1997.) Suffice it to say that I am overjoyed with the way that threads have been implemented in Java. The implementation is minimal and elegant. The simple way that methods can be protected from concurrent update, the equally simple semaphore and critical code mechanisms, the very easy way of creating a rendezvous between two threads, all combine to make this a good language feature.

OPERATOR OVERLOADING

While writing code in Java, I have to say that I miss being able to overload operators as in C++. This is not a critical issue, but I am disappointed.

TEMPLATES

Templates are a wonderful feature of C++. The fact that Java does not have them is of some concern to me. In Java, one cannot create a type-safe container. All containers in Java can hold any kind of object. This can lead to some ugly problems.

Mitigating these problems is the fact that all casts in Java *are* type safe. That is, Java casts are roughly equivalent to dynamic_cast of references in C++. An incorrect cast results in an exception being thrown. Since all objects coming out of a Java container must be downcast, and since such casts are relatively safe, the need for type safe containers is somewhat lessened.

```java
public void Notify()
{
    Enumeration i = itsObservers.elements();
    while(i.hasMoreElements())
    {
        Observer o = (Observer) (i.nextElement());
        // the cast above will throw an exception
        // if nextElement returns something
        // other than an Observer.
        o.Update();
    }
}
```

66 JAVA VS. C++

However, type safe containers are not the only good thing about templates. Templates in C++ are a very nice way of achieving static polymorphism. Consider the following C++ code:

```
template <class Modem>
void SendString(char* s, Modem& m)
{
    m.Dial("5551212");          // call my system.
    if (m.IsConnected())
    {
        while (*s)
            (m.Send(*s++);)
        m.Hangup();
    }
    else        // not connected
        cerr << "could not connect" << endl;
};
```

Here we see a C++ template function that employs static polymorphism. The SendString function can work with any class that has the methods: Dial, IsConnected, Send, and Hangup. Although it is more typical in both C++ and Java to gain this kind of polymorphism using abstract base classes, there are some distinct advantages to using templates. For example, there is no virtual overhead, i.e., no extra time or memory is spent managing the dynamic binding of normal C++ virtual functions.

For these reasons, I think that templates should be considered for later releases of Java.

LABELED BREAKS AND CONTINUES

OK, it's time for a minor rant. The language designers pride themselves on creating a language that does not have a goto statement. *(Design Patterns)* Yet, wonder of wonders, they added *labeled* break and continue. This is a sore point of mine. The tenets of *structured programming* do not disallow the use of goto. Rather they disallow its use in any context that destroys the single-entry/single-exit (SE/SE) paradigm. For example, using goto to create the equivalent of a for loop or a while loop does not violate structured programming. Of course in a language like C++ or Java it would be a silly thing to do, since those statements already exist.

The SE/SE paradigm says that every block of code should have a single entry point and a single exit point. There should be no way to enter such a block in the middle, and no way to exit such a block from the middle. Entry is at the top, and exit is at the bottom.

The use of break and continue in C, C++, or Java constitute a minor violation of SE/SE. We use them to transfer control out of the middle of a loop. The use of *labeled* break and *labeled* continue are a much more serious violation. These can be used to exit deeply nested blocks from their middles. Indeed, some of the enclosing blocks may not know that they are being exited and may be written to assume that they are not. This can lead to errors that are very hard to identify.

```
outer:
for (int i=0; i<99; i++)
{
    for (int j=0; j<99; j++)
    {
        if (AreWeDone(i,j) == true)
            break outer;   // get all the way out.
        else
            DoSomethingCool(i,j);
    }
    DoSomethingElse();
}
```

The code above shows a typical scenario. There are two nested loops, one iterating on i, and the other on j. In the inner loop, we test to see if some condition having to do with i and j will allow us to terminate the loop early. If so, we use a labeled break to exit both loops.

This example also demonstrates the danger of violating SE/SE. The outer loop expects to call DoSomethingElse every time the inner loop is finished. Yet the labeled break thwarts this. To correct this, we could use finally as follows:

```
outer:
for (int i=0; i<99; i++)
{
    try
    {
        for (int j=0; j<99; j++)
        {
            if (AreWeDone(i,j) == true)
                break outer;   // get all the way out.
            else
                DoSomethingCool(i,j);
```

68 JAVA VS. C++

```
        }
    }
    finally
    {
        DoSomethingElse();
    }
}
```

Or we could put the actual loop conditions in the inner for statement.

```
for (int i=0; i<99; i++)
{
    for (int j=0; j<99 && AreWeDone(i,j) == false; j++)
    {
        DoSomethingCool(i,j);
    }
    DoSomethingElse();
}
```

I make it one of my personal rules to avoid the use of break and continue as a way of managing loops. So I will probably not make much use of labeled break and labeled continue.

CONCLUSION

Java is a fun language. C++ programmers should have a relatively easy time learning it and will find that they enjoy using it. I have noted a few problems with the language in this article, but I don't consider these to be very critical issues. Moreover, I don't know of any language that doesn't have such problems. Language design always involves trade-offs that displease someone.

I look forward to writing lots of interesting Java applications. I also look forward to watching how the language evolves from this point onward. I expect to see some changes in the next few years.

Robert Martin is President of Object Mentor. He is also the author of the book *Designing Object-Oriented C++ Applications Using the Booch Method.* He can be reached at rmartin@oma.com.

URL
API for current version of Java
www.javasoft.com/products/JDK/
CurrentRelease/api

C++ vs. Java
Software Development

Barry Boone

RELAX. THIS IS not another article that compares Java and C++ feature by feature. That has already been done very well by others. Robert Martin provided a great comparison of key features of these two languages in the January, 1997 issue of *Java Report,* for example.

I'm after different game: How do Java's features affect the software development process as a whole? Does it feel the same to develop Java code instead of C++ code? What improvements can a technical manager expect to see from a *group* of programmers using Java instead of C++? How does the software development process change for the better by using Java instead of C++?

Sure, you still design, write, compile, test, deploy, and maintain your application. If you want to publish APIs, you can do that in either language. But underlying each development phase, the details are surprisingly different.

DESIGN

Designing in Java is simpler than designing in C++. This is mostly due to having to make fewer choices in Java; the language has already decided for you how you will approach your application.

If you're wary of Java, you'd say this is restrictive. If you're a fan, you'd say this is liberating. The reality is that many key questions are already answered for you before you ever sit with your team and start to hash out design issues. Each of the answers to these questions has the effect of making your design and your intent clearer. Here is a sampling:

69

70 Java vs. C++

What should be implemented using classes and what should be implemented using stand-alone functions and variables? In Java, there can be no functions or variables defined outside of a class. The class is the framework that everything is built on; classes define the outlines of your programs. This very first question affects your entire design approach. In Java, you begin to think about *what* you want to do, not *how* you want to do it. You begin to design classes, not functions. You think about APIs, not algorithms. This higher level of abstraction makes your designs better.

Which classes will be your base classes? Java's classes are *always* the base classes. If you do not specifically state which class a particular class will inherit from, that class will inherit from Java's Object class, which is at the root of all class hierarchies. This means that every class you design comes with a core set of capabilities—just look at the documentation for the Object class to see what they are. This also means that your objects can be used generically by other classes when they have to be. For example, a Queue class can be written to keep track of any Object subclass. This would mean it is capable of handling any object in your program, since all classes descend from Object.

Should a class inherit from multiple base classes? As many writers have already commented, Java has single inheritance of *implementation* and multiple inheritance of *interface*. With only single inheritance of implementation, it is impossible to set up conflicts and misunderstandings as to which set of behavior will overrule another.

How will control flow be altered if there is an error? Java insists that developers use exception handling. Methods *must* declare the exceptions they throw; callers *must* handle thrown exceptions.

How can I create subsystems made up of collections of classes so that I can reuse these classes easily in other applications? In Java, classes can be grouped into their own libraries, called packages. Once walled off into packages, classes can restrict access to their members by non-package classes more precisely and can make themselves usable by other classes in other applications.

Java's ability to produce a clean design is made clear by looking at three key building blocks of the language in comparison with C and C++. Java's designs are clean because Java enforces APIs. Without being able to access arbitrary memory locations, you cannot slip behind Java's back and circumvent the object-oriented paradigm. As you can see in Table 1, C++ extends C's capabilities by adding object-oriented features. Java breaks the connection with C's ability to crawl around in memory, retaining only C++'s object-oriented pieces.

Table 1. Language building blocks.

Building Block	C	C++	Java
Accessing memory	Pointers,	Pointers, addresses, objects	Objects
Grouping data	Structures	Structures, classes	Classes
Defining behavior	Functions	Functions, methods	Methods

IMPLEMENTATION

One of the biggest advantages of Java is also one that is not clearly apparent from a rundown of Java features. In Java, different programmers can work on different classes independently of each other much more easily than they can in C/C++.

In C/C++, there is a vast interdependence on files. One obvious interdependence is object files, which must be linked together to produce an executable. Another concerns header files; to enable classes, structures, constants, and other elements to be shared between files and programmers, programmers often define these things in header files. Figure 1 gives a sense of the file types that take part in the dance of C++ software development.

While header files and object files allow programmers to share classes, this capability comes at a steep price. Whenever a header file changes, all code that includes that header file is affected. Whenever an object file defining a superclass changes, all object files that define subclasses must be recompiled. This is because the layout of memory in a C/C++ program is determined at compile and link time—that is, before being run.

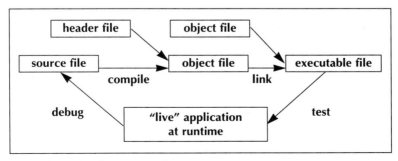

Figure 1. C/C++ development cycle.

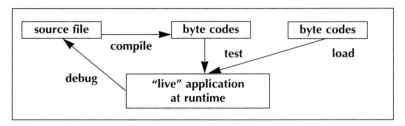

Figure 2. Java development cycle.

In Java, files and programmers are much more independent. First, there are no header files. Second, the compiled byte codes (Java's closest equivalent to object files) are loaded at runtime and assembled at runtime into a live, running application. Figure 2 provides an insight into this simpler dance.

This means that byte code or class files are less dependent on other ones. Memory is not determined at compile time, but *at runtime*. Files containing superclasses can change, and files containing subclasses do not need to be recompiled.

Another boon to implementation is relinquishing concerns about memory management, which is a primary source of bugs in C/C++. In Java, memory management bugs are almost completely eliminated because this is Java's responsibility. Others have written about Java's role with regards to garbage collection. But the feel of this is something else entirely.

Letting go of memory management runs counter to the instincts of most C/C++ programmers. Losing the reference to an allocated object stimulates exactly the same brain cells as throwing peanut shells on a barroom floor. You feel like you shouldn't be doing it, but you know that everyone else is, and you trust that someone will eventually come along and sweep them up. But that's the way it is in Java. Java is the janitor, and it's much handier with a broom than you will ever be.

The fact that Java takes over responsibilities that used to belong to the programmer is a key design philosophy of Java. Table 2 shows that the only responsibility the programmer retains from the tasks he was responsible for with C/C++ is writing good, creative code. The rest is now up to Java.

This is all very liberating and makes the development process go much quicker in Java. In fact, using APIs written by other programmers becomes

Table 2. Development responsibilities.

Responsible Party	C/C++	Java
Programmer	Good, creatively written programs Memory management Thread synchronization Platform specifics Error-handling protocols	Good, creatively written programs
Language	Grammar and syntax	Grammar and syntax Memory management Thread synchronization Platform specifics Error-handling protocols

much easier, precisely because Java enforces the implementation approach presented in Figure 2 (that is, how to access memory, group data, and define behavior).

Since Java manages the memory, something else occurs in addition to garbage collection: you cannot get around access restrictions, because you cannot get a pointer to an object and find arbitrary offsets into memory. Therefore, if a class declares a variable as private, it's private, by gum, and there's nothing you can do about it. This makes programmers stick to the APIs—because they have no choice!

Since Java provides the error-handling protocols, you cannot circumvent them. If a method might throw an exception, that method must state that this is the case in its declaration. If you invoke that method, you must supply error handling code surrounding that invocation. This again means that programmers stick to the APIs. There's no way around them.

With support for synchronized multitasking built into the language, multitasking is much easier in Java and enables new approaches to old problems. For example, imagine a server that listens on a port for incoming requests over the Internet. Without an easy way to implement concurrent processing, you might be tempted to queue or block other requests that arrive while you are scrambling to respond to the first client. With multitasking, you can spawn a lightweight process to handle that request and go back to listening on the port.

74   JAVA VS. C++

What's more, while there are multitasking libraries available, these are often platform-specific. Java is platform-independent. That means that your multitasking server software can run on a different server tomorrow when you decide to port your Web site to a different platform.

TESTING

How do programmers test their code, apart from system testing? In C/C++, programmers must jump through hoops to perform unit testing: create stubs, use different versions of the same code, and more. Java, however, has an elegant solution: each class can have its own main() method. This is impossible in C/C++ without a lot of conditional compilation, because in C/C++ there can be only one main() per executable. In Java, however, the main() the Java interpreter invokes is the main() belonging to the class you run.

So, instead of using the entire application to unit test your code, you can write a main() method for the class you want to test. This method can invoke methods in its class to verify that their output is as expected. And there's no need to remove these miscellaneous main() methods once the pieces are brought together until the very end, and then, only if the size of this test code becomes an issue.

The testing experience is also subtly different in Java than in C/C++. You will never run into problems where some symptom appears randomly, far away from the line of code that actually caused the problem in the first place. Why? Because:

- Garbage collection eliminates errors with freeing memory too soon or not soon enough.
- Bounds checking for arrays, and object references instead of pointers, eliminates accessing bogus memory locations.
- Strong type checking forces the programmer to not make assumptions.
- The need to initialize local variables eliminates flaky code that inadvertently uses a memory location's unknown state.

So, instead of testers finding new ways to frustrate programmers with results that cannot be reproduced, testers focus on looking for errors in an application's output and display. Testers become less concerned with crashing the application with wacky data, and more concerned with an application's results when run as intended. Errors resulting from wacky data are a cinch to find and fix; soon, these cases are eliminated completely.

DEPLOYMENT

There's a wonderful term called "forehead installation," where the installation process is so easy, all the user has to do is bang his forehead on the space bar (to click the "install" button already selected) and the software does the rest.

A Java program's ability to be deployed over a TCP/IP network as an applet is almost as simple. You can think of it as "forehead deployment." Since Java applets run in any Web browser, you can plug Java right into your intranet and use existing TCP/IP connections as your distribution model. How? Simply by placing the Java applet on your Web server and referencing it from a Web page. The Web browser will find the HTML references to your Java applet and pull it down from the server when needed.

Security protects your data and users. Java's security arises from three sources:

When run as an applet within the context of a Web browser, byte codes are first verified by the Java runtime environment and security manager to make sure they are legal and have not been tampered with. In particular, Java byte codes refer to methods by names, not by offsets, as with C/C++. These names are verified by the Java runtime—something that is impossible to do with the offsets in a C/C++ program. Memory is laid out only after the byte codes have been verified, just before the program is about to run. This makes it impossible to execute arbitrary memory locations, and so it is virtually impossible to write a virus.

When the runtime environment finally executes the applet, it runs the applet within a carefully fenced-in region of memory. The restrictions are quite strict. For example, the applet cannot get access to the file system, nor can it access a server other than the one it came from.

Because Java manages the memory, Java programs cannot even inadvertently access memory they are not supposed to. Because illegal memory access will throw an exception and shut down the offending thread if the exception is not caught, buggy code will not wreak havoc with a user's machine.

76 JAVA VS. C++

MAINTENANCE

Ease of maintenance depends on three things:

1. A clear design
2. A streamlined way to redistribute changed software
3. A well-documented design

We've already discussed how Java helps make your design clear. And redistributing a Java applet is as simple as posting it on the server; the clients' Web browsers will simply retrieve the new version the next time it's needed. Now let's turn to documentation.

In C/C++, the typical way to document classes and their fields and functions is by adding comments to the header files the classes are defined in. This is dangerous, because the implementation can change somewhere in a source file, resulting in the documentation back in the header file being wrong.

In Java, there are no header files. What's more, there is no separation between a method declaration and its implementation. Unlike in C/C++, there is no such thing as a forward declaration of a method; a method's code is defined in place with its declaration. But this does not mean you have to wade through source code to find comments. The standard Sun version of the Java Development Kit defines a tool (called *javadoc* in Sun's JDK) that scans Java source files and produces pretty HTML files of your classes, methods, and variables, all hyperlinked and ready to view in your favorite Web browser. What's more, if you place these HTML files in the same directory as Java's own APIs, links in these files reference Java's own classes, where appropriate (in little diagrams of class hierarchies).

This approach allows you to publish your APIs, for yourself and others, without spending time managing separate headers or documentation files. With this documentation tool, you can still distribute your compiled classes and hide their implementations.

Java even defines a special code comment that javadoc searches for and places into the HTML files it generates. This allows you to add your own special comments to the nicely structured class, method, and variable names and references that javadoc generates on its own.

CONCLUSION

This article explained how to run that familiar, complex steeple chase from design to maintenance more swiftly and easily with Java compared with C++. We looked at Java's benefits in the software development process, including a clearer architecture and design, a simpler development cycle, more robust code, a "forehead deployment," and easier maintenance. If you haven't explored Java development already, I hope you and your programming team soon have the opportunity to experience all these benefits for yourselves.

Barry Boone is the author of *Java Essentials for C and C++ Programmers* and *Learn Java on the Macintosh,* with Dave Mark. Both books are published by Addison-Wesley. Barry performs contract programming and Java training. He can be reached at barryb@bluehorse.com and maintains a Web site at http://www.learnjava.com.

SECTION FOUR

AWT

Answering Frequently Asked AWT Questions

David Geary

IN THIS ARTICLE, we'll take a look at a few of the most frequently asked questions concerning the AWT from comp.lang.java.programmer. Certain AWT questions cycle endlessly through the newsgroup and therefore are worthy of our attention here.

FORCING A LAYOUT

It is not uncommon for situations to arise in which it is necessary to force a container to layout its components. Since the recipe for programmatically forcing a layout is not readily apparent, how to force a layout qualifies as a frequently asked question.

Figure 1 shows the applet from Listing 1 in action—a simple panel with a textfield and two buttons for adjusting the textfield's font size. Changing the font size results in an immediate update in the textfield's font, but the textfield does not grow or shrink to accommodate the text it displays, as you can see from Figure 2. We would like the applet to behave as depicted in Figure 3, that is, we would like the container in which the textfield resides to be forced to layout out its components whenever we change the textfield's font size. This will result in dynamic feedback of the size of the textfield as we change the font size.

All components, at any given time are either valid or invalid. Invalid components need to be laid out; valid components do not. Calling validate() on a container that is invalid (and whose peer has been created) results in a call to the container's layout() method. (Remember that last sentence.)

81

82　AWT

```
Listing 1.

import java.applet.Applet;
import java.awt.*;

public class ValidateApplet extends Applet {
    private GrayPanel grayPanel = new GrayPanel();
    public void init() {
        add(grayPanel);
    }
}
class GrayPanel extends Panel {
    private TextField  field     = new TextField  ("TextField");
    private Button     lgButton  = new Button     ("larger font");
    private Button     smButton  = new Button     ("smaller font");

    public GrayPanel() {
        add(field);
        add(lgButton);
        add(smButton);
        setBackground(Color.gray);
    }
    public boolean action(Event event, Object what) {
        if(event.target instanceof Button) {
            Button button   = (Button)event.target;
            Font   curFont   = field.getFont();
            int    newSize   = curFont.getSize();

            if(event.target == lgButton) newSize += 3;
            if(event.target == smButton) newSize -= 3;

            field.setFont(new Font(curFont.getFamily(),
                        curFont.getStyle(), newSize));
        }
        return true;
    }
    public void paint(Graphics g) {
        g.setColor(Color.black);
        g.drawRect(0,0,size().width-1,size().height-1);
    }
}
```

So our job is relatively easy, as you can see from the modified action()
method for the GrayPanel class in Listing 2. After setting the field's font,
we invalidate the field, and then invoke validate() on the GrayPanel's
parent (container).

Realize that we never explicitly invalidated the parent (container) of
the GrayPanel, although we did explicitly validate it. Remember that a
call to validate() for a container will only result in a call to layout() if the
container itself is invalid. How then, did the GrayPanel's container get

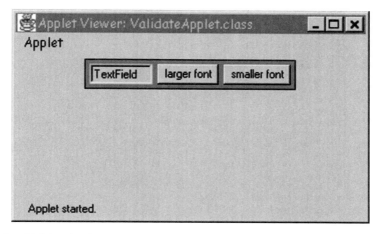

Figure 1. ValidateApplet.

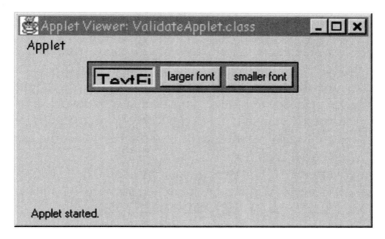

Figure 2. ValidateApplet without forced layout.

invalidated? Invalidating an AWT component invalidates not only the component itself, but the container in which it resides. Note that since the container is also a component, it behaves in a similar manner—invalidating itself, and invalidating its container. Thus an invalidate() call on a component can actually walk up the container hierarchy and invalidate all the containers in its path. As a result, our call to field.invalidate() invalidated not only the field, but the field's container and every container up through the applet and culminating at the applet's frame.

84   AWT

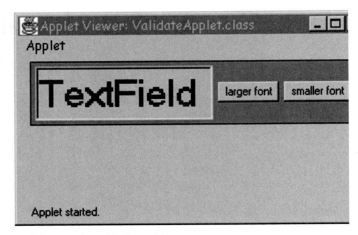

Figure 3.   ValidateApplet with forced layout.

Finally, it should be noted that invalidation of a component occurs naturally as a side effect to a number of Component methods, namely: show(), hide(), reshape(), resize(), add(), remove() and setLayout(). Since setFont() is not one of the methods listed, setting the field's font will not invalidate the field, so we have to do it manually by invoking field.invalidate(). If, however, you call one of the Component methods that invalidate as a side effect in addition to setting the font, then the explicit call of field.invalidate() is no longer necessary.

Another related FAQ concerns resizing a Window or Dialog in response to a change in size of a component contained in the window or dialog. Listing 3 introduces two classes: ValidateDialog, which contains an instance of GrayPanel and LaunchPanel, an extension of GrayPanel that adds a button for launching a ValidateDialog. Since GrayPanel calls validate() on its container, we override the dialog's validate() method, where we resize the dialog to accomodate the preferred size of the dialog's GrayPanel. Figures 4 and 5 show the dialog before and after the font size has been changed.

ACCESSING A COMPONENT'S FRAME

If you comb the source for the AWT classes looking for a setCursor() method, you will currently find it in only one place—the Frame class. As an aside, note that the set Cursor() method will also make an appearance

ANSWERING FREQUENTLY ASKED AWT QUESTIONS   85

Listing 2.

```
public boolean action(Event event, Object what) {
    if(event.target instanceof Button) {
        Button button    = (Button)event.target;
        Font    curFont   = field.getFont();
        int     newSize   = curFont.getSize();

        if(event.target == lgButton) newSize += 3;
        if(event.target == smButton) newSize -= 3;

        field.setFont(new Font(curFont.getFamily(),curFont.getStyle(), newSize));

    // Setting the font of the TextField (field) does not invalidate the
    // TextField, so we must do it manually.

        field.invalidate();

    // We validate our parent (container) which will cause us to be laid out:
        getParent().validate();
    }
    return true;
}
```

in the Component class in version 1.1 of the AWT, and will take an argument of type Cursor instead of an int; in the meantime, if you want to change the cursor for a component, you have to go through its frame.

As a result, one of the most frequently asked AWT questions is "How do I change the cursor inside my applet?" since an applet does not extend Frame. Another frequently asked question is "Where do I get a reference to a frame to pass to a dialog constructor?"

The answer to these questions is quite straightforward, as long as you realize one fundamental concept: *all* components must reside inside of a frame. An applet, for instance, resides in either a Java-enabled browser or the appletviewer, both of which reside in a frame. The only challenge remaining, then, is to find the frame associated with an applet. Listing 4 shows a class from the Graphic Java Toolkit that contains a number of utility methods, one of which is Frame getFrame (Component). The Util.getFrame() method simply walks up the hierarchy of containers until it discovers an instanceof Frame, and then returns a reference to the frame. As another aside, the Graphic Java Toolkit (GJT) is a toolkit of custom components built on top of the AWT, such as image buttons, separators, bar gauges, image filters, scrollers, and a sprite animation

Listing 3.

```java
import java.applet.Applet;
import java.awt.*;

public class ValidateApplet extends Applet {
    private LaunchPanel launchPanel = new LaunchPanel();
    public void init() {
        add(launchPanel);
    }
}
class GrayPanel extends Panel {
    private    TextField    field        = new TextField ("TextField");
    private    Button       lgButton     = new Button        ("larger font");
    private    Button       smButton     = new Button        ("smaller font");

    public GrayPanel() {
        add(field);
        add(lgButton);
        add(smButton);
        setBackground(Color.gray);
    }
    public void paint(Graphics g) {
        g.setColor(Color.black);
        g.drawRect(0,0,size().width-1,size().height-1);
    }
    public boolean action(Event event, Object what) {
        if(event.target instanceof Button) {
            Button button    = (Button)event.target;
            Font    curFont = field.getFont();
            int     newSize  = curFont.getSize();

            if(event.target == lgButton) newSize += 3;
            if(event.target == smButton) newSize -= 3;

            field.setFont(new Font(curFont.getFamily(),
                        curFont.getStyle(), newSize));

            // Setting the font of the TextField (field) does not
            // invalidate the TextField, so we must do it manually.

            field.invalidate();

            // We validate our parent (container) which will cause us to be
            // laid out:
            getParent().validate();
            }
            return true;
        }
    }

class LaunchPanel extends GrayPanel {
    private Button              launchButton = new Button("launch ...");
    private ValidateDialog   validateDialog;

    public LaunchPanel() {
        add(launchButton);
    }
    public boolean action(Event event, Object what) {
        if(event.target == launchButton) {
            if(validateDialog == null) {
                validateDialog = new ValidateDialog(gjt.Util.getFrame(this),
                "Validate Dialog  ",   true);
            }
            validateDialog.show();
                return true;
        }
        return super.action(event, what);
    }
}

class ValidateDialog extends Dialog {
    public ValidateDialog(Frame frame, String title, boolean modal) {
        super(frame, title, true);
        add("Center", new GrayPanel());
        pack();
    }
    public void validate() {
        super.validate();
        resize(preferredSize().width, preferredSize().height);
    }
    public boolean handleEvent(Event event) {
        if(event.id == Event.WINDOW_DESTROY) {
            dispose();
            return true;
        }
        return super.handleEvent(event);
    }
}
```

Answering Frequently Asked AWT Questions   87

```java
package git;

import java.applet.Applet;
import java.awt.*;

/**
 * A handy collection of methods for getting a component's
 * frame, getting a component's applet, waiting for a
 * component's image, and wallpapering a components back-
 ground.
 * <p>
 *
 * @version 1.0, Apr 1 1996
 * @author David Geary
 */

public class Util {
    public static Frame getFrame(Component component) {
        Component c = component;

        if(c instanceof Frame)
            return (Frame)c;

        while((c = c.getParent()) != null) {
            if(c instanceof Frame)
                return (Frame)c;
        }

        return null;
    }
    public static Dialog getDialog(Component component) {
        Component c = component;

        if(c instanceof Dialog)
            return (Dialog)c;

        while((c = c.getParent()) != null) {
            if(c instanceof Dialog)
                return (Dialog)c;
        }

        return null;
    }
    public static Applet getApplet(Component component) {
        Component c = component;

        if(c instanceof Applet)
            return (Applet)c;

        while((c = c.getParent()) != null) {
            if(c instanceof Applet)
                return (Applet)c;
        }

        return null;
    }
    public static void waitForImage(Component component,
                    Image image) {
        MediaTracker tracker = new MediaTracker(component);
        try {
            tracker.addImage(image, 0);
            tracker.waitForID(0);
        }
        catch(InterruptedException e) { Assert.notNull(null); }
    }
    public static void wallPaper(Component component,
                    Graphics g,
                    Image image) {
        Dimension compsize = component.size();
        Util.waitForImage(component, image);

        int patchW = image.getWidth(component);
        int patchH = image.getHeight(component);

        Assert.notFalse(patchW != -1 && patchH != -1);

        for(int r=0; r < compsize.width; r += patchW) {
            for(int c=0; c < compsize.height; c += patchH)
                g.drawImage(image, r, c, component);
        }
    }
    public static void setCursor(int cursor,
                    Component component) {
        getFrame(component).setCursor(cursor);
    }
    public static void beep() {
        System.out.write(7);
        System.out.flush();
    }
}
```

88 AWT

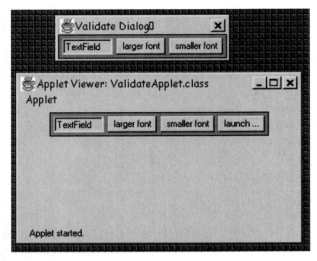

Figure 4. ValidateDialog initially launched.

package. The GJT is freely available; and if you wish, you may download it as follows:

```
ftp.prenhall.com
login as anonymous
use your name as password
cd pub/ptr/sunsoft_books.w-053/geary/ graphic_java
```

Anyway, getting back to the question at hand, remember that an applet is a component, by virtue of the fact that it extends Panel, which extends Container, which in turn, extends Component. Therefore, in order to change an applet's cursor, you must simply find its frame, and then invoke setCursor() on the frame, like so:

```
import java.awt.*;
import java.applet.Applet;
import gjt.Util;

public class MyApplet extends Applet {
    public void init() {
        Frame myFrame = Util.getFrame(this);

myFrame.setCursor(Frame.WAIT_CURSOR);
    }
}
```

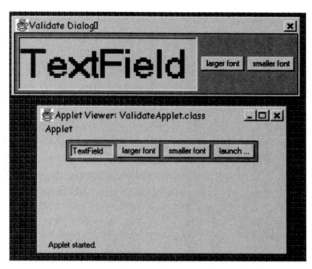

Figure 5. ValidateDialog with large textfield font.

If you paid close attention to the methods in the gjt.Util class in Listing 4, however, you'll realize that we don't need to go through all the hassle of finding the frame associated with the applet, as the gjt.Util class provides a setCursor(int, Component) method which takes care of that headache for us. As a result, setting the cursor for an applet becomes a simple matter:

```
import java.awt.*;
import java.applet.Applet;
import gjt.Util;

public class MyApplet extends Applet {
   public void init() {
      Util.setCursor(Frame.WAIT_CURSOR, this);
   }
}
```

As yet another aside to this topic, it is good practice to set an applet's cursor to the wait cursor in the init() method, and then change it back to the default cursor in the start() method. This is due to the fact that some applets take some time to load, especially when run in a browser through a modem, and therefore it's a nice touch to let your users know that you're actually doing something (instead of just sitting in limbo), while

90   AWT

the applet is loading. In fact, it might behoove you to implement an extension of Applet that does the above, from which you can extend your applets, similar to the applet in Listing 5. When you implement your own applet class and extend MyApplet, you simply call super.init() and super.start() first thing in your overridden init() and start() methods, respectively.

Finally, note that the gjt.Util class in Listing 4 also contains similar methods for obtaining a reference to the dialog or applet associated with a component. Realize, however, that although every component must reside in a frame, not every component must reside in an applet or a dialog, so those methods can potentially return a null reference.

PEER CREATION

Our final topic addresses the creation of a component's peer. This topic actually comes up in a number of frequently asked AWT questions, such as:

1. When I'm creating an offscreen buffer, why do I keep getting a null reference?
2. Why is the size of my component (0,0)?
3. Why do I get a null reference for my component's font?

Almost without exception, such questions are the result of invoking a createImage(), size(), or getFont() method on the applet, respectively, before the component's peer has been created.

The AWT retains native look and feel by adopting a peer approach. Each AWT object, such as Button, Checkbox, and Panel, actually do very little on their own; most of their behavior is delegated to a native GUI

Listing 5.

```
import java.applet.Applet;
import java.awt.*;
import gjt.Util;

public class MyApplet extends Applet {
    public void init() {
        Util.setCursor(Frame.WAIT_CURSOR, this);
    }
    public void start() {
        Util.setCursor(Frame.DEFAULT_CURSOR, this);
    }
}
```

ANSWERING FREQUENTLY ASKED AWT QUESTIONS   91

Listing 6.

```
package java.awt;
import java.awt.peer.PanelPeer;

public class Panel extends Container {
    final static LayoutManager panelLayout = new
FlowLayout();

    public Panel() {
        setLayout(panelLayout);
    }
    public synchronized void addNotify() {
        peer = getToolkit().createPanel(this);
        super.addNotify();
    }
}
```

component. For instance, an AWT Button has a Windows button as its peer under Windows 95/NT, and has a Motif button as its peer under Solaris. In fact, if you look at the source for java.awt.Panel, you will notice that there is virtually nothing to a panel at all; nearly all of its functionality is implemented by a native peer. Listing 6 shows the source for the 1.02 version of java.awt.Panel with all of the commentary stripped out.

Peers are somewhat of a double-edged sword for the AWT. On the one hand, they allow applets to retain the native look and feel of whatever platform the applet is being displayed on, and additionally, they enabled rapid development of the AWT, since the original implementors of the AWT did not have to reinvent all of the functionality for each component from scratch. On the other hand, peers obfuscate the implementation of AWT components, and make it difficult to extend the functionality provided by AWT components, as one would typically expect to do with an object-oriented toolkit.

Listing 7 shows an applet that contains an extension of Panel. MyPanel, tries to discover its size, get a reference to its font, and create an offscreen image in its constructor, after which it prints out the respective values of each. The output of the applet shown in Listing 7 is as follows:

```
Panel size:    java.awt.Dimension[width=0,height=0]
Panel font:    null
Offscreen:     null
```

The offscreen buffer and the font are null and the size of the panel is (0,0) because, at the time of construction, the panel's peer has not yet been

92   AWT

Listing 7.

```java
import java.applet.Applet;
import java.awt.*;

public class Test extends Applet {
    public void init() {
        MyPanel panel = new MyPanel();
        setLayout(new BorderLayout());
        add("Center", panel);
    }
}
class MyPanel extends Panel {
    Image  offscreen;
    Font   myFont;
    Dimension mySize;

    public MyPanel() {
        offscreen = createImage(100,100);
        myFont    = getFont();
        mySize    = size();

        System.out.println("Panel size:  " + mySize);
        System.out.println("Panel font:  " + myFont);
        System.out.println("Offscreen:   " + offscreen);
    }
}
```

created. As we have alluded to, much of a component's functionality is delegated to its peer, and creating offscreen buffers, reporting the component's size, and obtaining access to a component's font are all delegated to a peer. As a result, due to the fact that the component's peer has not yet been created, we get useless values from each call.

Of course, the solution to the problem is simply to wait until the peer is created, before attempting to perform any functions that are delegated to the peer. When can we be assured that a component's peer has been created? The first thing that might occur to you is that the peer must be created when the paint() method is called, otherwise there would be nothing to paint into, and you would be correct. In fact, if you look at Listing 8, you will see that we have moved the calls to create the offscreen image, and access the panel's font and size to an overridden paint() method, and from the output below, you can see that we have indeed been successful:

```
Panel size:   java.awt.Dimension [width=500,height=300]
Panel font:   java.awt.Font[family=Dialog,
              name=Dialog,style=plain,size=12]
Offscreen:    sun.awt.win32.Win32Image @46c1fc
```

However, there are times when it is simply not possible to wait for paint() to be called without accessing some functionality that is delegated to a peer. For instance, we may need to access a component's font in order to make certain calculations that must be done before paint() is invoked. In such a case, we may override the method that creates the peer itself: addNotify(). Listing 9 shows the same functionality moved to the addNotify() method. addNotify() is invoked by the underlying AWT machinery when it is time for a component to create its peer—in fact, you can see the implementation of java.awt.Panel.addNotify() if you refer to Listing 6. Notice that after the panel has created its peer, it invokes its superclass addNotify, to ensure that the superclass peer has been created. This is typical of all AWT components; they first create their peer, and then invoke super.addNotify(). In our extension of Panel, note that we call super.addNotify() before doing anything else, as it is the call to super.addNotify() that actually creates the component's peer. Once the peer has been created, then we can go about creating the offscreen buffer, and accessing the font and size information. Note that it is absolutely essential that you also call super.addNotify() anytime you override

Listing 8.

```
import java.applet.Applet;
import java.awt.*;

public class Test extends Applet {
    public void init() {
        MyPanel panel = new MyPanel();
        setLayout(new BorderLayout());
        add("Center", panel);
    }
}
class MyPanel extends Panel {
    Image offscreen;
    Font   myFont;
    Dimension mySize;

    public void paint(Graphics g) {
        offscreen = createImage(100,100);
        myFont   = getFont();
        mySize   = size();

        System.out.println("Panel size: " + mySize);
        System.out.println("Panel font: " + myFont);
        System.out.println("Offscreen:  " + offscreen);
    }
}
```

94 AWT

Listing 9.

```java
import java.applet.Applet;
import java.awt.*;

public class Test extends Applet {
    public void init() {
        MyPanel panel = new MyPanel();
        setLayout(new BorderLayout());
        add("Center", panel);
    }
}
class MyPanel extends Panel {
    Image offscreen;
    Font   myFont;
    Dimension mySize;

    public void addNotify() {
        super.addNotify();

        offscreen = createImage(100,100);
        myFont    = getFont();
        mySize    = size();

        System.out.println("Panel size:  " + mySize);
        System.out.println("Panel font:  " + myFont);
        System.out.println("Offscreen:  " + offscreen);
    }
}
```

addNotify(), or the peer's component will never get created, which can lead to some very interesting and undesirable results. Finally, note that we can also call addNotify() directly to force the creation of the component's peer; however, that can sometimes be a risky business, due to the fact that the component's container must have a peer before the component can force its own to be created. As a result, direct calls to addNotify() can result in NullPointerExceptions being thrown. The safer approach is to override addNotify(); then you know it's being called at the correct time.

Life Span of an Applet

Henry Wong

IN THIS ARTICLE, we'll examine the life span of an applet. When we create an applet by deriving from the Applet class, we sometimes forget that we are creating a new class and the browser will be creating a new instance of that class. The Applet class also derives from the Panel class, which derives from the Container class which, in turn, derives from the Component class. This means that the applet we create is also a component, container, and panel in AWT. And of course, an applet object is supposed to represent an applet that is on the HTML page. The applet that we create has a life span as a class; a life span as an object; a life span as an AWT component, container, and panel; and finally, a life span as an applet on a Web page with a life span of its own. These are the many life spans that we will examine in this installment. (At the time of this writing, the current JDK is version 1.0.2. However, the information presented in this article should also apply to JDK 1.1).

```
void start()
void stop()
```

An applet—like gif, jpeg, or any other visible component on the Web page—may only be important during the intervals that it is visible. In order to help an applet determine this interval, the browser will call the start() and stop() methods of the Applet class. The start() method is called when the applet is to begin its visible interval and the stop() method is called when the applet is to end its visible interval. The applet should allocate resources and activate the tools needed in the start() method; it should deactivate or deallocate the resources in the stop() method.

In Listing 1, the BounceCount applet does many tasks during this visible interval. Whenever the interval is started, the start() method will increment the count and generate a new string that will be displayed. The

96 AWT

Listing 1.

```
import java.awt.*;
import java.applet.*;

public class BounceCount extends Applet {
    private Color c;
    private Font f;
    private FontMetrics fm;

    private int count;
    private String s;
    private int x, y;
    private Thread tx, ty;

    public void init() {
        count = 0;
        c = Color.blue;
        f = new Font("TimesRoman", Font.BOLD, 24);
        fm = getFontMetrics(f);
    }

    public void start() {
        count++;
        s = "counter=" + count;

        int minx = 0;
        int miny = fm.getAscent();
        int maxx = size().width - fm.stringWidth(s);
        int maxy = size().height - fm.getDescent();
        x = minx; y = miny;
        tx = new ShakerThread(10, this, 0, minx, maxx);
        tx.start();
        ty = new ShakerThread(15, this, 1, miny, maxy);
        ty.start();

    }

    public void stop() {
        tx.stop();
        ty.stop();
    }

    public void paint(Graphics g) {
        g.setColor(c);
        g.setFont(f);
        g.drawString(s, x, y);
    }

    public synchronized void shake(int ref, int value) {
        if (ref == 0) {
            x = value;
        } else {
            y = value;
        }
        repaint();
    }

}

public class ShakerThread extends Thread {
    private int interval, id;
    private BounceCount applet;
    private int min, max, current, change;
    public ShakerThread(int t, BounceCount b,
                        int r, int m, int M) {
        interval = t; applet = b; id = r;
        min = m; max = M;
        current = min; change = 1;
    }

    public void run() {
        while (true) {
            try {
                sleep(interval);
                current += change;
                if (current > max) {
                    current = max; change = -1;
                }
                if (current < min) {
                    current = min; change = 1;
                }
                applet.shake(id, current);
            } catch (InterruptedException e) {}
        }
    }

}
```

start() method also calculates the borders of the string in order to bounce the string within the borders of the applet. The actual bouncing of the string is done by two other threads that will oscillate the *x* and *y* coordinates. Since the two bounce threads are only necessary when the applet is visible, they are created and started in the start() method and stopped in the stop() method.

The applet does not have to be visible for the start() method to be called. The applet may be covered by another window or may be scrolled off of the Web page. Current browsers tie the visible interval to the visible interval of the Web page. The start() method will be called when the page is shown, whether it is a new page or one that is in the cache. The most common cache is the history cache. This is the cache that holds the pages that can be revisited with the "back" and "forward" buttons. Current browsers also start() and stop() the applet when the browser is deiconified and iconified, respectively. This last behavior is relatively new. In any case, applet developers should not write applets that depend on when in particular the start() and stop() methods are called in order to function correctly.

```
void init()
void destroy()
```

The interval between the init() and the destroy() methods is what many regard as the true life span of the applet. The init() method is called when the applet is first loaded and instantiated, and the destroy() method is called just prior to the applet being discarded. Unlike the start() and stop() methods, these methods will only be called once per instance.

In Listing 1, the init() method creates the font, font metrics, and color that we will use in the applet. We could have also accomplished this in the start() method (or even in the paint() method), but since there is no harm in creating these resources earlier, we place these calls in the init() method. Another reason we do this is because we would also like to allocate these resources only once. There is no need to deallocate these resources in the destroy() method, since the resources will be dereferenced when the applet gets dereferenced.

When this interval occurs, the applet does not have to be in the browser's history cache. It is perfectly fine for the browser to keep the applet in a different cache if the browser has the resources to support the applet. This will allow the browser to simply restart the applet if the user reloads the Web page (via a bookmark, or the "go" menu). It is also okay for the browser to destroy() an applet that is in the history cache in order to free up resources. If this applet is needed again, it will simply be reloaded and initialized. Applet developers should not write applets that depend on the particulars of when the init() and destroy() methods are called to function correctly.

AN APPLET IS A CLASS AND AN OBJECT

To create an applet, we have to derive from the Applet class and include our specific code. We have to introduce a new class that will have to be

98   AWT

downloaded. Once this class is downloaded, an instance of the class will then be created. This means that our applet has the life span of a class as well as an object. This allows us to have static initializers, constructors, and even a finalizer in our applet.

In Listing 2, we have a ButtonApplet that contains two Buttons, and a ButtonPanel that also contains two Buttons. Both the ButtonApplet and ButtonPanel require that the layout manager be set and the Buttons added. However, the ButtonPanel accomplished this in the constructor while the ButtonApplet accomplished it in the init() method. This is because the ButtonPanel is not an applet and hence does not have an init() method. The act of setting the layout manager and components in the container is simply configuring data structures. Setting these values in the constructor when they are known is generally the best solution. Whether the applet developer chooses to add components in the init() method or in the constructor of the ButtonApplet is purely personal preference. It may be preferable for the applet to be consistent with all the panels and to add the components in the constructor. However, it may not be preferable to have both a constructor and init() method in the applet. It is not possible to move all the tasks from the init() method to the constructor.

Listing 2.

```
import java.awt.*;
import java.applet.*;

public class ButtonApplet extends Applet {
    Component n, m, s;

    public void init() {
        setLayout(new BorderLayout());
        add("North", n = new Button("Top of Applet"));
        add("South", s = new Button("Bottom of Applet"));
        add("Center", m = new ButtonPanel());
    }
}

class ButtonPanel extends Panel {
    Component n, m, s;

    public ButtonPanel() {
        setLayout(new BorderLayout());
        add("North", n = new Button("Top of Panel"));
        add("South", s = new Button("Bottom of Panel"));
        add("Center", m = new Panel());
    }
}
```

LIFE SPAN OF AN APPLET 99

Many resources—getImage(), getAudioClip(), getCodeBase(), etc.—are not available until the init() method is called.

As for the static initializer and the finalizer, there is little reason to have either. Since only one instance of the applet is created, there is little reason to do something in the static initializer that could not be accomplished in the constructor or the init() method. There is also no reason to create a finalizer, since any task can be accomplished in the destroy() method.

An Applet is an AWT component.

```
void addNotify()
void removeNotify()
```

Since the applet derives from the Panel class of AWT, it can be treated like a panel, container, or component. And just like any component of the AWT, it has a particular life span. This life span is determined by the addNotify() and removeNotify() methods. For components, this is very important when it needs to access resources from the windowing system as early or as late as possible. For the Applet, this may not be necessary, since the applet has the init() and destroy() methods. The scope of the component is larger than the scope of the applet. The applet is a usable component before it is initialized and is destroyed before it is no longer a component. However, developers may want to move windowing-specific initialization and destruction of resources to the addNotify() and removeNotify() methods to be consistent with all components.

In Listing 3, we now have the windowing-specific resources allocated in the addNotify() method. If we had to deallocate those resources, we could also have placed them in the removeNotify() method. For these simple resources, this is not necessary. We could have allocated them as early as the constructor. In the case of the FontMetrics class, it is not usable until the applet is in component scope. Older versions of the JDK will also return a null in the getFontMetrics() method. Operations that are more involved with the windowing system like setting the cursor or controlling the resizability of the window are better suited for these methods. (It is my personal preference to use only the init() and destroy() methods for these resources in an applet, and to either use the constructor or delay using the resource for any other component.)

Unlike the other methods that we can override, the addNotify() and removeNotify() methods actually have tasks to accomplish. The overriding method must call the original methods. In our addNotify() method,

100   AWT

Listing 3.

```java
import java.awt.*;
import java.applet.*;

public class BounceCount extends Applet {
    private Color c;
    private Font f;
    private FontMetrics fm;

    private int count;
    private String s;
    private int x, y;
    private Thread tx, ty;

    public void addNotify() {
        super.addNotify();
        c = Color.blue;
        f = new Font("TimesRoman", Font.BOLD, 24);
        fm = getFontMetrics(f);
    }

    public void init() {
        count = 0;
    }

    public void start() {
        count++;
        s = "counter=" + count;

        int minx = 0;
        int miny = fm.getAscent();
        int maxx = size().width - fm.stringWidth(s);
        int maxy = size().height - fm.getDescent();
        x = minx; y = miny;
        tx = new ShakerThread(10, this, 0, minx, maxx);
        tx.start();
        ty = new ShakerThread(15, this, 1, miny, maxy);
        ty.start();
    }

    public void stop() {
        tx.stop();
        ty.stop();
    }

    public void paint(Graphics g) {
        g.setColor(c);
        g.setFont(f);
        g.drawString(s, x, y);
    }

    public synchronized void shake(int ref, int value) {
        if (ref == 0) {
            x = value;
        } else {
            y = value;
        }
        repaint();
    }
}
```

LIFE SPAN OF AN APPLET   101

we must call the super classes' addNotify() method. Technically, the component is not attached to the windowing system until the super classes' method is called. (This is not exactly true, but it is best envisioned this way.) This means that if we need component-related resources, we should allocate them after calling super.addNotify() in the addNotify() method. This also means that we can accomplish tasks before the component is attached by placing the code before the super.addNotify() method call.

MISCELLANEOUS AND CONCLUSION

We have examined the applet throughout its many life spans. The Applet that we create is a class, an object, a component in AWT, and of course, an applet. There is however, one scope that does not fit into any of these life spans. This is because an applet is only one of many that may exist on the HTML page. Just because one applet has loaded and is being initialized does not mean that all of the applets for that page have completed loading. This affects the getApplet() method that is used to establish applet to applet communications.

In Listing 4, the StockTicker applet needs to obtain a reference to the StockReader applet. Even though this can be done in the init() method, it is done in the start() method in order to give more time for the StockReader

```java
Listing 4.

import java.io.*;
import java.awt.*;
import java.applet.*;

public class StockTicker extends Applet {
    private StockReader sr;
    private InputStream is;

    public void start() {
        do {
            // The StockReader should be defined in the
            // HTML page with "STOCKSOURCE" as-
signed
            // as its name
            sr = (StockReader)
                getAppletContext().getApplet("STOCK-
                    SOURCE");
        } while (sr == null);
        is = sr.getStockFeed();
    }
}
```

102 AWT

applet to load. Even so, there is no guarantee that the other applet has loaded, and the start() method must loop until the StockReader applet has actually loaded. (There are other issues like security and whether the other applet actually exists that are beyond the scope of this article.)

This concludes our examination of applets. Hopefully, in the next applet that we create, we will treat the applet as not only an applet, but a class, an object, and a component as well. At the very least, keeping data-specific portions of the applet with the object, and keeping the window-ing-specific portions of the applet with the component, will help keep some consistency with the other objects and other components contained in the applet. For those who don't totally agree—of which I am one—this study should help in the separation of the different identities of the applet, and help provide a better understanding of the many applet resources.

SECTION FIVE

PATTERNS

Applying Design Patterns in Java

Erich Gamma

THE IDEA OF PATTERNS has progressed rapidly from cult to mainstream status. Several pattern catalogs (*Design Patterns—Elements of Reusable Object-Oriented Software,* by Gamma et al., and *Pattern-Oriented Software Architecture—A System of Patterns,* by Buschmann et al.) are available, and there are conferences that focus on writing patterns: PLoP— Pattern Languages of Programs (*Pattern Languages of Program Design,* by Coplien and Schmidt and *Pattern Languages of Program Design 2,* by Vlissides et al.), and EuroPLoP. Another new conference is called UP and focuses on using patterns (available on the Web as UP—An International Conference on Using Patterns).

Patterns occur at different levels of abstraction (see *Pattern-Oriented Software Architecture,* by Buschmann). At the lowest level are patterns that describe programming language idioms. They demonstrate how to use particular features of a programming language. The next level up are design patterns, which describe teams of communicating objects and classes. Design patterns are sometimes referred to as micro-architectures that contribute to the overall architecture of a system. At the highest level of abstraction, one finds architecture patterns for designing the system architecture. This article focuses on design patterns exclusively.

JAVA AND DESIGN PATTERNS

In principle, design patterns are independent of the programming language. They can be implemented in standard object-oriented languages. However, a good pattern description provides hints for implementing the

106 PATTERNS

pattern in a particular language. This is what makes them accessible and applicable.

Despite its popularity, Java is still relatively young and hints for leveraging Java-specific properties are missing from most pattern descriptions. The following Java features promise to have the greatest impact on existing pattern descriptions:

- *Interfaces:* Many design patterns promote clean separation of interface and implementation. In Java, interfaces can be defined independently of the class hierarchy or of inheritance relationships.
- *Packages* give you precise control over the visibility of classes. Several design patterns can profit from this language feature by using it to hide implementation classes from clients.
- *Final methods and classes:* Methods and classes can be marked as final. They become final in the sense that they cannot be redefined or extended in subclasses. This does not just enable optimizations and ensure security; a developer can also document which components in the system are not designed for extension.

In addition, support for garbage collection and access to meta information (java.lang.Class) is of importance for the implementation of design patterns.

From the design-patterns perspective, Java is interesting for yet another reason. The Java-API has a high "pattern density," and the applied patterns are relatively easy to identify. Using the Java-API by way of example, this article shows how design patterns can be leveraged during the design, redesign, and the communication of a design.

DESIGN

To begin, we'll concentrate on the Java Abstract Window Toolkit (AWT) and do some "reverse design," i.e., we'll reconstruct the design process to demonstrate the use of design patterns.

One of the exceptional characteristics of Java is the platform independence of its applications. It handles dialog elements such as buttons or input fields (in AWT called components) that have different dimensions on different platforms. As a consequence, positioning components by specifying absolute coordinates is problematic: What may look good on one platform can appear pretty chaotic on another.

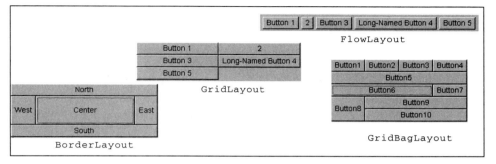

Figure 1. Possibilities supported by AWT.

AWT solves this problem by letting you position elements declaratively. Elements are positioned by using one of several layout algorithms. For example, a FlowLayout asks its components for their preferred size and arranges them left to right until no more components fit on the same line. There are multiple strategies for arranging components, each with its own trade-offs. Figure 1 illustrates some of the possibilities that AWT supports.

AWT's Container class is responsible for grouping components. An obvious solution is to implement different layout policies as container subclasses (e.g., FlowLayoutContainer, BorderLayoutContainer). However, there are already Container subclasses for different container kinds such as Panel and Window. We want to be able to use layout policies independently of the container kind. If the layout algorithms were defined in Container subclasses, then this would not be possible. Inheritance forces us to choose a particular base class. To summarize, we have the following design problem:

- There are different layout policies.
- Container classes must be able to use different layout policies.
- Clients have to be able to configure which layout policy a container uses.

Design patterns help us find a suitable solution for such a problem. Reviewing the problems addressed by available patterns, the Strategy pattern springs to mind. The strategy pattern, as described in the catalog, has the following intent:

> Define a family of algorithms, encapsulate each one, and make them interchangeable. Strategy lets the algorithm vary independently from the clients that use it.

The strategy pattern's solution distinguishes two roles:

- A strategy that encapsulates the algorithm behind an interface
- A strategy context that maintains a strategy object and delegates the implementation of the algorithm to its strategy object

As a consequence, the algorithm can be combined with an arbitrary context. In our example, the algorithm corresponds to a layout policy, which is implemented by a LayoutManager. Figure 2 shows the solution implemented in AWT using the strategy pattern. The figures follow a convention that annotates a class with the role it plays in a design pattern. A LayoutManager is assigned to a container using setLayout. The method layout starts the layout process. LayoutManager defines the interface common to all layout policies. It is defined as a Java interface. As this example shows, the strategy interface can be defined as an interface when implementing the Strategy design pattern in Java. A consequence of using an interface instead of an abstract class is that it cannot provide any default behavior.

A container is only dependent on the interface defined by LayoutManager and can work with all layout policies, which implement this interface. It is even possible to swap the layout policy dynamically at runtime.

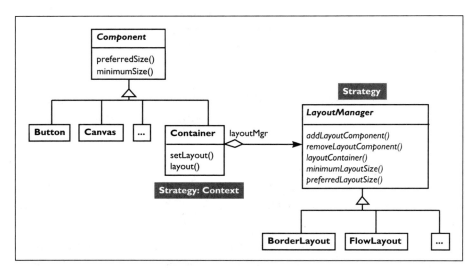

Figure 2. Solution implemented in AWT using the strategy pattern.

When implementing the strategy pattern, the design of the communication between context and strategy is of particular interest. The algorithm encapsulated in the LayoutManager requires access to input parameters, such as the container and its components. One possibility is that the container passes all necessary parameters to the LayoutManager as arguments to the layout method. By doing so, the LayoutManager is decoupled from the Container. However, it is difficult for the Container to know what parameters a particular LayoutManager might need. It risks passing too little or too much information.

An alternative approach is to pass the Container itself as a parameter to the layout method. If Container provides sufficient accessing methods, a LayoutManager can determine the parameters from Container. This is the solution used by AWT. The call in Container is as follows:

```
Container.layout() {
//...
    layoutMgr.layoutContainer(this);
}
```

Another interesting variation is when a LayoutManager implementation doesn't store a Container-specific state. In this case, you can share a single LayoutManager for numerous Containers, thereby reducing the number of LayoutManagers needed at runtime. An example for this is FlowLayout. By default, a Panel uses a FlowLayout as its LayoutManager. FlowLayout objects do not themselves store any container-specific state information and can therefore be shared by many containers. The corresponding FlowLayout object is created once and shared among all Panels.

Not all LayoutManagers are sharable; for example, BorderLayout keeps references to the Components of the Container it has to lay out. It is therefore tied to a specific container. As a consequence it is not sharable. The pattern behind the FlowLayout design variation is the Flyweight pattern. The Flyweight pattern addresses the problem of reducing the number of objects that have to be created. The solution suggested by Flyweight involves extracting the object-specific state information from the object and passing it as parameters to the object. The object itself can then be shared. Designing objects such that they are sharable is an important design strategy to reduce the number of fine-grained objects in a system.

In Java, object sharing is greatly simplified thanks to automatic garbage collection. In particular, a developer need not be concerned with whether an object is shared or not.

110   PATTERNS

REFINEMENT AND REDESIGN

Design patterns help refine and improve existing designs. There are situations in which the components of a container should not be automatically arranged. For such situations, AWT allows a container's LayoutManager to be set to null:

```
Panel panel = new panel;
panel.setLayout(null);
```

Hence, the use of a LayoutManager is optional, and the container tests whether a LayoutManager is set. If it isn't, then the container does not automatically arrange its components. As a consequence the Container code is sprinkled with numerous conditional statements. The methods layout, add, remove, removeAll, preferredSize, and minimumSize all follow the same scheme:

```
if (layoutMgr != null)
    layoutMgr.layoutContainer(this);
```

These additional execution paths add to the code complexity. It is always desirable to minimize the number of execution paths. How could the code in the AWT Container be simplified? Here too a design pattern comes in handy: the Null Object design pattern (EuroPLoP Proceedings 1996, and PLoP Proceedings 1996).

Null Object solves this problem by defining an object for the null case, which has no behavior. We eliminate the if expression and replace it with polymorphic behavior that does nothing. So in this example we introduce a NullLayout class that implements the LayoutManager interface with no behavior (see Listing 1).

NullLayout objects have no state and like FlowLayout they can be shared. To manage the single shared NullLayout object, we apply the Singleton pattern. The intent of the Singleton pattern states:

Ensure a class only has one instance, and provide a global point of
    access to it.

Using the Singleton pattern, a class maintains a single instance in a static class variable that can be accessed by a corresponding static accessing method. We therefore add the code shown in Listing 2 to the class NullLayout.

APPLYING DESIGN PATTERNS IN JAVA   111

Listing 1.

```
public class NullLayout implements LayoutManager{
    public void addLayoutComponent(String name, Component comp) {}
    public void removeLayoutComponent(Component comp) {}
    public Dimension preferredLayoutSize(Container target) {
        // return the current Container size
    }
    public Dimension minimumLayoutSize(Container target) {
    // return the current Container size
    }
    public void layoutContainer(Container target) {}
}
```

Listing 2.

```
public class NullLayout implements LayoutManager{
    private static final NullLayout singleton = new NullLayout();
    public static LayoutManager getLayout() {
        return singleton;
    }
    private NullLayout () {}
    //...
}
```

The constructor is declared as "private" to prevent clients from creating additional NullLayout objects. With all this in place the code to turn off automatic layout becomes:

```
Panel panel = new Panel;
panel.setLayout(NullLayout.getLayout());
```

COMMUNICATION

Design patterns are not only useful during design and redesign, they also greatly facilitate the communication of a design. Design patterns define a vocabulary for discussing a design.

AWT uses several design patterns. If developers are familiar with these patterns, then their understanding of the design and properties of an

112 PATTERNS

architecture like AWT is improved. In particular, the way it is designed to be extended can be better understood. Several examples will demonstrate this, always assuming that the reader is familiar with the corresponding design patterns.

AWT allows components to be grouped together to create complex dialog elements. Its designers applied the Composite pattern to this end. The Container class manages components and is itself derived from Component; that is, it performs the role of Composite.

AWT uses the Strategy pattern discussed earlier to allow flexible configuration of a container's layout policy.

In AWT events can be handled in a hierarchical way. Multiple components get a chance to handle an event. As a consequence the sender and the receiver of an event are decoupled. This is an example of the Chain of Responsibility pattern. According to this pattern, an event is propagated from the leaves to the root in the component hierarchy, until a component handles the event.

While the Java-API is platform-independent, it uses platform-specific widgets internally. This fact is hidden from clients using the Bridge pattern. Component objects hold a "Peer" object, whose interface is defined by a Peer interface, which in turn provides the connection to the platform-specific widget. In the context of the Bridge pattern, the Peer corresponds to the implementation, and Component corresponds to the abstraction (see Fig. 3).

For each Component class, there is a corresponding Peer interface. For example, a Button uses the ButtonPeer interface. Peer interfaces must be implemented for all supported platforms. The ButtonPeer interface is implemented under Motif by the class MotifButtonPeer and under Windows by the class Win32ButtonPeer.

Peer interfaces permit different component implementations for different platforms. This begs the question, how is an appropriate Peer implementation for a particular Component selected at runtime? This is where the Abstract Factory pattern gets into the act. The class Toolkit is an abstract factory. It defines methods for the creation of Peer objects (see Fig. 4).

Subclasses of Toolkit ensure that the correct Peer objects are created on a particular platform. For example, the Win32Toolkit implements the factory methods so that Peer objects for the Windows platform are created.

When implementing the Abstract Factory pattern, you need to decide how the abstract factory itself should be created. Every direct dependency

APPLYING DESIGN PATTERNS IN JAVA   113

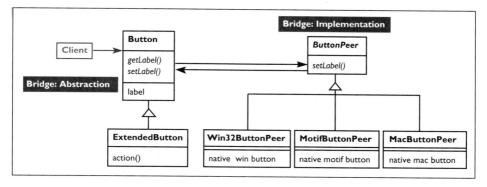

Figure 3.   Peer corresponds to the implementation.

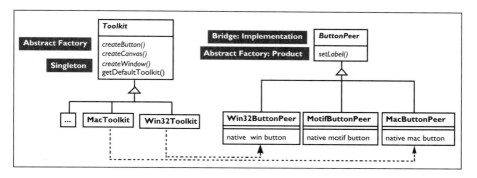

Figure 4.   Abstract Factory gets into the act.

in code to a class such as Win32Toolkit must be avoided. The Java runtime system can help us here. Rather than hard-coding the class name, it can be determined from configuration data as a string. Using this string, the corresponding Class object can be found using the static method Class.forName. Once you have the class object, you can create the appropriate factory object (see Listing 3). The class Toolkit is itself an Singleton. The static method getDefaultToolkit provides access to its sole instance.

The Java-API exposes only the abstract class Image to clients. Concrete implementations of Image, such as GIFImage, are not visible. This is possible because the creation of an image is performed by Factory Methods.

To this end, the class Applet provides a method getImage and the class Component provides createImage. This is a good example of how factory methods can be used to hide implementation classes.

114 PATTERNS

Listing 3.

```
String toolkitName = // e.g. "sun.awt.motif.Mtoolkit");
Class toolkitClass = Class.forName(toolkitName);
Toolkit toolkit = (Toolkit)toolkitClass.newInstance();
```

Together, all of these examples demonstrate how design patterns can cover a sizable chunk of an architecture. Particularly interesting is how the patterns applied in AWT all intersect in its Component class, which becomes a focal point for the design. This is a common phenomenon: cooperating design patterns yielding one or more classes that participate in multiple patterns. For example, Component and Container are involved in the Composite, Strategy, Bridge and Abstract Factory design patterns.

Design patterns are useful throughout the software development lifecycle, including initial design, redesign, communication, and documentation.

Erich Gamma has been discovering and working with design patterns for the past seven years. Currently he is an architect and senior consultant at IFA Consulting in Zürich, Switzerland (www.ifa.ch). He is co-author of *Design Patterns—Elements of Reusable Object-Oriented Software*. He can be reached at gamma@ifa.ch.

URLs
UP—An International Conference On Using Patterns
http://www.panix.com/~k2/up.html

Patterns and Java Class Libraries

Iseult White

DESIGNING REUSABLE object-oriented software is hard. To be reusable, the design must be specific enough to address the problem at hand and general enough to support future requirements. This article takes a look at the role that patterns play in designing reusable software in Java and shows how abstract classes, interfaces, and concrete classes collaborate in a framework that implements a particular design pattern.

Design patterns capture good solutions to recurring design problems. These solutions have been used over and over in many different systems. The pattern captures the design at an abstract level. Examples of patterns can be implemented in different languages, and even in different ways. The Java class libraries implement a number of design patterns. The FilterStream classes are examples of the Decorator Pattern. Component and Container implement the Composite pattern. LayoutManager embodies the Strategy pattern. In this article we are going to examine how Enumeration and Dictionary from java.util embody the Iterator patterns.

Frameworks, on the other hand, are implementations of reusable designs in a specific language. The framework defines the overall structure, and the key responsibilities of the classes that collaborate to provide the framework. You reuse the framework by subclassing abstract classes in the framework, and providing specific implementations to address your needs.

Four elements are necessary to describe design patterns. The pattern Name is a handle used to describe the problem being solved. The Problem describes situations where the pattern is applicable. The Solution defines

116 PATTERNS

the elements that make up the design, their relationships, responsibilities, and collaborations. The Consequences are the results and trade-offs of applying the pattern.

Let us take an example, the Iterator pattern. Iterator provides a way to access the elements of a collection sequentially without exposing the collections underlying representation. The classes Dictionary and Enumeration of java.util implement the Iterator pattern. Here is a description of each of the classes that collaborate in this pattern. Figure 1 and the following list shows the relationships between them.

- Dictionary is an abstract class that defines the operations for managing Dictionary objects and defines the interface for creating an Enumeration object.
- Enumeration is an interface. It defines the basic iteration capabilities of the Iterator pattern. It allows clients to traverse the Dictionary an element at a time until the traversal is complete.
- Hashtable is a concrete class that provides a hash table implementation of the Dictionary class. It implements the Enumeration creation interface to return an instance of the HashtableEnumerater.
- HashtableEnumerater is a concrete class that implements the Enumeration interface in terms of the HashTable class.

The goal of this pattern is to take responsibility for access and traversal out of the Dictionary class and put it into an Enumeration object. The function elements() of Dictionary returns an Enumeration object. Through repeated calls to the nextElement() method in Enumeration, we can traverse each element in the Dictionary. The Enumeration object keeps track of the current position in the traversal.

The consequences of this pattern are:

- It supports variations in the traversal of the Dictionary. Different subclasses can provide different styles of iteration.
- Enumeration simplifies the interface of the Dictionary class. The Dictionary class provides operations for the insertion and removal of elements, but does not address traversal.
- More than one traversal can be pending on a Dictionary.

The iterator pattern incorporates another very useful pattern, the Factory Method. The factory method defines an interface for creating an object, but lets subclasses decide which class to instantiate. Clients of the Dictionary request an Enumeration object through the elements() method. The concrete subclass is responsible for creating and returning the correct instantiation of Enumeration. Hashtable is an example of a concrete class. It returns a HashtableEnumerator object. The factory method pattern allows clients of Dictionary to write code that is independent of the concrete class they are using. The Factory method approach gives rise to two class hierarchies, one for the Dictionaries, and another for Enumeration classes. The elements() factory method connects the two hierarchies.

Now we are going to apply the Iterator pattern to define a List and Iterator hierarchy. Figure 2 shows this hierarchy. The implementation of the List class exposes the key concepts involved in building frameworks. It also highlights some of the issues involved in reusing code that already exists. The following classes are in the List hierarchy:

- AbstractList is an abstract class that defines the operations for managing Lists and defines the interface for creating a ListIterator object.
- ListIterator is an interface that extends the Enumeration interface. Enumeration is a consume once form of iteration. Clients can reset the ListIterator and use it again.
- ArrayList and SkipList are concrete classes that provide alternate implementations for the List class.
- ArrayListIterator and SkipListIterator are concrete classes that implement the ListIterator interface in terms of their associated concrete list classes.

Listing 1 shows a partial listing for AbstractList and ArrayList. On line 11 we see the declaration of the abstract Factory method createIterator(). On line 33 we see the implementation of this function in the concrete class ArrayList. This function creates an object of the concrete class ArrayListIterator and returns it. Line 31 of Listing 2 shows the code for the ArrayListIterator constructor. The ArrayListIterator maintains a reference to its parent list myList, and it sets its cursor to point to the first element in myList.

Line 19 of Listing 1 shows the append(object o) function of AbstractList. This function implements common code for the append function for all subclasses of list. Line 20 checks if the list is full and throws the ListFullException if it is. If the list is not full then the protected abstract function doAppend(Object o) is called on line 21. Subclasses override

118 PATTERNS

Figure 1. Iterator and factory patterns in dictionary and enumeration.

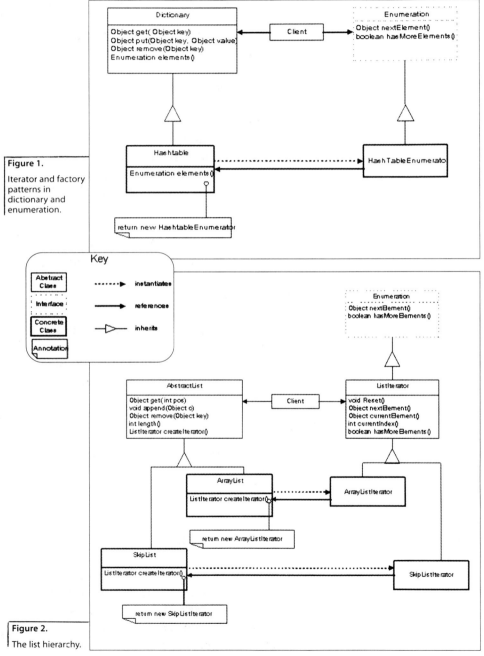

Figure 2. The list hierarchy.

PATTERNS AND JAVA CLASS LIBRARIES   119

Listing 1.

```
01 package Lists;
02 import java.lang.*;
03 import java.util.*;
04
05 public abstract class AbstractList {
06 /*  *
07     * Factory method which creates an Iterator for the
08     * list. Subclasses override this method to create
09     * the appropriate concrete iterator.
10     */
11     public abstract ListIterator createIterator();
12 /*  *
13     * appends an object to the end of the list
14     * @param o is the object to be appended
15     * @exception throws ListFullException if the list
16     * has reached its capacity.
17     * @Subclasses: Implement doAppend() to provide
              append() functionality.
18     */
19     public void append(Object o) throws ListFullException {
20         if (myLength == size) throw new
           ListFullException() ;
21             doAppend(o);
22             myLength++;
23     }
24 /*  *
25     * subclasses should implement this function to
              provide append
26     * functionality.
27     * @param o is the object to be appended
28     */
29     protected abstract void doAppend(Object o);
30     protected int myLength = 0;// current length of the
           list
31 }
32 public class ArrayList extends AbstractList {
33     public ListIterator createIterator(){
34             return (ListIterator) new ArrayListIterator(this);
35     }
36     protected void doAppend(Object o){
37         list[myLength] = o;
38     }
39 /*  *
40     * Package level interface which allows iterators
              implement iteration functionality
41     */
42     Object list[];
43 }
```

120 PATTERNS

Listing 2.

```
01 public abstract interface ListIterator extends Enumeration{
02 //   The iteration scheme is:
03 //   ListIterator i = someListObject.createIterator();
04 //   while(i.hasMoreElements){
05 //       (i.nextElement())    .//process this element
06 //       (i.currentElement())  .// do more processing to this element
07 //   }
08 /*  *
09    * sets the Iterator back to the beginning
10    */
11    abstract public void reset();
12 /*  *
13    * returns the next element in the list and advances iterator
14    */
15    abstract public Object nextElement() ;
16 /*  *
17    * returns the current element in the list but does not advance iterator
18    */
19    abstract public Object currentElement() ;
20 /*  *
21    * returns true if there are more elements
22    */
23    abstract public boolean hasMoreElements();
24 /*
25    * returns the index of the current element. This allows clients to
26    * remove element from list by using the remove(int i)
27 */
28    abstract public int currentIndex();
29 }
30 class ArrayListIterator implements ListIterator{
31    ArrayListIterator(ArrayList list){
32        myList = list;
33        cursor = 0;
34    }
35    public void reset(){ cursor = 0; }
36    public Object nextElement(){
37        if (myList.length() == 0) throw new NoSuchElementException();
38        return myList.list[cursor++];
39    }
40    public Object currentElement(){
41        if (myList.length() == 0) throw new NoSuchElementException();
42        return myList.list[cursor];
43    }
44    public boolean hasMoreElements(){ return ( cursor < myList.length());}
45    public int currentIndex(){
46        return (cursor - 1);
47    }
48    protected ArrayList myList;
49    protected int cursor;
50 }
```

this function to provide the appropriate append functionality for their implementation. Line 36 shows where ArrayList implements doAppend (Object o). SkipList would implement doAppend(Object o) for a skiplist representation.

This shows how to use abstract classes, abstract functions and protected functions to create a framework. The superclass does as much work as it can, and then delegates to the subclass when it is finished. The difference between reuse in a framework and reuse in a class library is that there is an inversion of control between the client and the methods that it calls. When you use a class library, you write the main body and call the methods you want to reuse. When you use a framework you reuse the main body, and write the methods it calls. The List example is fairly trivial but demonstrates how to extend this paradigm to more complex frameworks.

The next issue to look at is maintaining semantic consistency when extending the Java class libraries. We have to pay attention to the exceptions thrown by the classes we inherit from. For example Enumeration.nextElement() throws a runtime exception NoSuchElement Exception. Runtime exceptions do not have to be handled in a try clause, but classes that implement Enumeration should maintain the semantic consistency of Enumeration. On lines 37 and 41 of Listing 2 we see the methods nextElement() and currentElement() doing just that.

In the preceding paragraphs we have seen how classes, interfaces, and instances interact to implement a number of design patterns in Java. Design patterns are a wonderful tool for understanding the complexities of object-oriented designs and implementations. Understanding the patterns implemented by the Java Class libraries will help you to create highly reusable and robust code.

Iseult White works at Catalyst Solutions, a premier provider of Java training. She can be reached at iseult@catalyze.com, or on the Web at http://www.catalyze.com.

Singleton

Dwight Deugo and Allen Benson

THE PROBLEM FOR this pattern discussion is a simple one—how can you ensure that a class has only one instance and how can you access that single instance?

CONTEXT

In nearly every system that we help clients develop, there are requirements to store and retrieve information from one or more databases. Although object-oriented databases are ready for "prime time," many of our clients still use relational databases. Using a relational database with an object-oriented language results in a well-known problem called the *impedance mismatch problem*. Relational databases are very good at storing information as rows in tables. However, objects do not, in all cases, map directly onto a row in a single table. Complex objects, such as an insurance policy, require many rows in different tables. This problem has forced developers to design and implement objects called *brokers* that handle the assembling of business objects from tables on read requests and the disassembling of these objects on write requests. There are many patterns dealing with brokers, but we'll leave those for another issue.

A broker's responsibilities often include connecting and disconnecting from a database. These actions enable the broker to setup its internal state to, for example, enable object caching. If a broker supports object caching, it will not read an object from the database if it has read it before. It simply returns the one it cached. Depending on the type of system you are developing, you can see a significant performance benefit using object caching in your broker.

124   PATTERNS

Broker object caching raises an interesting question. How many instances of a broker should one have in a system? If there is more than one, there are an equal number of object caches. Multiple caches defeat the purpose of object caching because the same request given to two different brokers will result in two instantiations of the object from the database. How is one to ensure that their system uses one and only one instance of a broker?

This situation is not unique. There are many cases where you want only one instance of an object used in a system. Take, for example, an object that manages the opening and closing of all windows. Since this object must know which windows are open, it will not want another window manager opening any others. What about the object that represents the system you are building? Would you want two system objects in your system? This creates one of those questions the philosophers can argue about for years: Which system object does the system use? Or, which system object maintains the system object?

A slightly different situation is when you want only one instance of any window open at one time. In this case, you do not want to ensure that the same instance is always used, but you want to make sure there is never more than one instance in existence at one time. This is a common requirement. For example, you do not want to develop a system that permits one to open several identical edit windows on the same business object. This causes a problem because, often, users forget that they had previously opened an edit window. Permitting them to open another, and another, not only leads to many open windows, it forces them to perform a merge operation once they discover the duplicate editors. A better solution is to have every request to open a window bring the user's focus back to the same window they previously opened. This is a job for a window manager, which itself should be a solitary instance.

We'll focus our attention to the first situation where we want to permit one and only one instance of a class in the system for the life of the system. The pattern for this situation is called the Singleton (*Design Patterns: Elements of Reusable Object-Oriented Software*, E. Gamma et al, 1995).

SOLUTION

This pattern's solution is equally simple. It is the instance class' responsibility to create, maintain, and provide a method for other objects to obtain a reference to the only instance. In addition, the class must stop other objects from creating instances of itself. The class is not responsible for what its instance does. This responsibility belongs with the instance.

The distinction between an instance and a class is important. Too often we see people confuse the difference. They are both objects, and, as a result, can be sent messages. However, they are different objects and support different message protocols. Think of a class as an object that builds things: e.g., a factory. Think of an instance as what a factory builds. You would never ask a car to build another one. However, you would go to a car factory and ask it to build a car for you. Make sure you are not asking your classes to perform operations that should really be done by their instances or vice versa!

Listing 1 describes an example implementation that uses the Singleton pattern. The implementation is for a GenericSystem object that can be extended to meet the requirements of any future system. Our runtime application needs only one instance of this object operational. To ensure a single instance of a GenericSystem class within an application we begin by defining the private class variable singleton on line 2. The variable is declared private to force objects to use the singleton() access method defined on line 11. The singleton() method creates a new instance of GenericSystem and assigns it to the singleton class variable if an instance does not already exist, and then returns the instance assigned to the variable. This form of variable initialization is known as lazy initialization and guarantees that the instance is created and initialized once—on the first access.

For this example, we wanted our instance to keep track of how often it was accessed. This number is incremented every time a request is made for the default instance of the GenericSystem and stored in the instance's instance variable, accessRequests, defined on line 4. If we defined the singleton variable public, any object could modify or access it directly and we would not be able to maintain the number of times an access is requested. By creating it as a private variable and adding the class access method singleton(), these problems are avoided.

We also provided a releaseSingleton() class method to allow other objects to reset the singleton. In our example, this method only sets the singleton class variable to null. In other implementations of this pattern, you will find that your releaseSingleton() method will need to perform additional housekeeping activities, such as clearing other system values. The control of what to release belongs with the object that owns the single-ton object—the GenericSystem class—not with the many different objects

126 PATTERNS

```
Listing 1. Generic System Class.

1.  public class GenericSystem extends Object {

        /* Class Variable */
2.      private static GenericSystem singleton;

        /* Instance Variables */
3.      public String userName;
4.      public int accessRequests;

        /* Constructor Methods */
5.      private GenericSystem() {
6.          userName = "<Unknown>";
7.          accessRequests = 0;}

8.      private GenericSystem(String name) {
9.          this();
10.         userName = name;}

        /* Class methods */
11.     public static GenericSystem singleton() {
12.         if (singleton == null)
13.             singleton = new GenericSystem("Java Man");
14.         singleton. accessRequests = singleton. accessRequests + 1;
15.         return singleton;}

16.     public static void releaseSingleton() {
17.             singleton = null;}

        /* Instance Methods */
18.     public String toString() {
19.         return (userName + " " + accessRequests);}
20. }
```

that use the singleton. This way, if you have to change the releasing behavior, you only have to change it in one place.

In Java, you can create instances of the class by sending it the new message. Since we do not want other objects creating instances of the GenericSystem class, we implemented the corresponding constructor methods as private, shown on lines 5 and 8. These methods can be used by the class (lines 9 and 13) but other objects will not be able to get past trying to compile the line: new GenericSystem() or new GenericSystem ("Some String").

The barrier is complete. To access an instance of GenericSystem, objects must send the class the message singleton(). Our Generic System-Test class, shown in Listing 2, tests our implementation. It makes three requests to the GenericSystem for its default instance and prints the

SINGLETON 127

Listing 2. Generic System Test Class.

```
1.  import java.io.*;

2.  public class GenericSystemTest extends Object{

        /* Class Methods */
3.      public static void main(String argv[])throws IOException {
4.          GenericSystem system;

5.          system = GenericSystem. singleton();
6.          System.out.println(system);

7.          system = GenericSystem. singleton();
8.          System.out.println(system);

9.          system = GenericSystem. singleton();
10.         System.out.println(system);

11.         System.out.println("Enter any character to end test");
12.         System.in.read();}
13.}
```

Listing 3. Output From Generic System Test Class.

```
Java Man 1
Java Man 2
Java Man 3
```

instance to standard output. As shown in Listing 3, the output is from the same instance of the GenericSystem. The only difference is that the access requests are incremented, which was what we asked the instance to maintain.

DISCUSSION

You will see example implementations of the Singleton pattern where the instance is not maintained by the class, but, rather, its protocol is provided as part of the class' protocol. The class, which there can only be one of, represents the singleton. Java's System class is one such example. It provides access to the system and runtime environment resources.

128 PATTERNS

Using only a class to implement the singleton pattern has some disadvantages. First, it makes it difficult to modify the implementation in the future to permit more than one instance. This change in requirement happens! We met one group who used the class approach to access their one database broker object. Of course, they later found out that they had to reference two databases and they needed two brokers.

Another disadvantage is that, since static class variables are not inherited in Java, implementing the Singleton pattern in a subclass of the original singleton can be difficult.

From reading about the Singleton pattern in this issue, we hope you have begun to think about other pattern problems: How to maintain a single instance at any one time, not for the entire life of the system? How to maintain a fixed number of instances? How to manage several different types of singletons? These are patterns that we will talk about in time.

SECTION SIX

TECHNIQUES

How to Drag and Drop Images

Jeremy Sevareid

DRAG AND DROP is a powerful user interface gesture found in the Mac OS, Windows 95, and Motif interfaces, among others. One of its most common uses is visual file management: deleting files by dropping their icon into a "trash can" or moving files and folders by dropping them into other folders. This article presents an example of how to drag and drop an image within an applet using the Java AWT library.

JAVA VERSUS CGI—
A DRAG-AND-DROP EXAMPLE

Drag and drop is one way in which Java can add significant value over HTML/CGI. To users who have grown accustomed to applications with sophisticated user interfaces, web applications based on HTML and CGI seem crippled by comparison.

The closest that HTML forms and CGI can get to drag and drop can be seen in the Mr. Potato Head builder. There a user chooses a nose, mouth or hat by clicking on its radio button. Then the user clicks on a specific spot on Mr. Potato Head's image. Both parameters are passed to a CGI script, which generates a new GIF file on the fly and returns it to the user's browser. Not only is the form's interface awkward, but the round-trip from browser to the server and back again required by CGI is slow.

Compare this to the Java version of Mr. Potato Head. A user can drop noses, lips, and eyes into place intuitively and quickly. Java is clearly superior to HTML/CGI for applications that need a drag and drop interface.

131

THE DESIGN

This sample implementation creates an applet that lets the user drag and drop an image within the applet. This is done with an abstract base class, Draggable, a derived class, DraggableImage, and the applet.

Draggable knows how to drag something, but not how to draw it or where its boundaries lie. Because Draggable is abstract, it cannot be instantiated, but classes derived from it can be. Draggable is abstract because it lacks implementations for two methods, isTouching and draw. It leaves the coding of those methods up to the derived class.

DraggableImage knows how to draw an image and gauge if a point falls within its borders. DraggableImage derives from Draggable and implements the two abstract methods, isTouching and draw. By extending Draggable, DraggableImage provides the applet with a way to drag and drop an image.

This division of labor between base and derived class makes it easy to create new items that can be dragged and dropped. Simply write a new class that extends Draggable and implements the two abstract methods. The new class need only know how to detect if an x–y coordinate is within its borders and how to draw itself on the screen; Draggable takes care of the rest. The result is a new item that can be dragged and dropped.

The applet loads the image and handles the mouse actions. It instantiates a DraggableImage, which lets the applet use both the base and derived classes' functionality.

THE FLOW OF CONTROL

Here's how the three pieces work together: The user clicks somewhere on the applet, invoking the applet's mouseDown. It calls DraggableImage's isTouching to check if the mouse click happened within the boundaries of the image. If so, then mouseDown calls Draggable's startDrag, letting the image know it's being dragged.

As the user drags, the applet's mouseDrag method gets passed the new x–y coordinates. mouseDrag calls Draggable's setPosition, which stores the new and old positions. Then mouseDrag calls repaint. This invokes Draggable's paint function, which erases the image at the old position and then draws it at the new one. Finally, when the user releases the mouse button, the mouseUp method of the applet gets called, which invokes endDrag, leaving the image at the most recent coordinates, effectively dropping it there.

THE CODE

Now let's examine the code in detail, following the flow of control outlined above. The applet's init method gets called first (lines 8–18) (see Listing 1 for the applet's listing). It uses AWT's MediaTracker to wait until the GIF file is completely loaded into the Image instance before going on (lines 10–14). It then instantiates a DraggableImage object, passing it a reference to itself and the fully loaded image. Finally, it sets the starting screen position of the image.

The important thing about DraggableImage's constructor (lines 10–14) is that it calls Draggable's constructor (line 11) (see Listing 2 for DraggableImage's listing and Listing 3 for Draggable's listing). That enables Draggable to initialize itself (lines 13–18). By setting drawn to true (line 17), Draggable's constructor stops paint (lines 40–55) from displaying the image before the initial coordinates are set by the applet.

XORMODE

Once init is done, the applet's paint method gets called (lines 20–22). It invokes Draggable's paint method (lines 40–55). Notice the call to setXORMode (line 44). This is the key to how paint draws and then erases the image while it's being dragged across the screen. If something is drawn while XORMode is on, then drawing it again in the same place with XORMode on will erase it and restore what was underneath. So, on this initial call to paint, the image will be drawn in XORMode so the image can be erased later when the user drags it somewhere else.

The paint method then calls DraggableImage's draw method (lines 24–27), which does the actual work of displaying the image on the applet, completing the applet's paint call.

THE DRAW AND ERASE CYCLE

Now, onto how a drag and drop happens step-by-step. When the user clicks, the applet's mouseDown method is called (lines 24–31). It passes DraggableImage's isTouching method the x–y coordinates of the click. isTouching returns true if the coordinates are within the boundaries defined by the rectangular shape of the image (lines 16–22). If the click is within bounds, Draggable's startDrag is called. That method sets a boolean flag, being_dragged, indicating that the image is being dragged (line 20).

134 TECHNIQUES

Listing 1.

```
01 import java.awt.*;
02
03
04 public class test extends java.applet.Applet {
05
06     DraggableImage di;
07
08     public void init(){
09
10         // wait until the image is loaded
11         Image i = getImage(getCodeBase(), "image.gif");
12         MediaTracker tracker = new MediaTracker(this);
13         tracker.addImage(i, 0);
14         try { tracker.waitForAll(); } catch (Exception e) {}
15
16         di = new DraggableImage(this, i);
17         di.setPosition(new Point(0,0));
18     }
19
20     public void paint(Graphics g) {
21         di.paint(g, getBackground());
22     }
23
24     public boolean mouseDown( Event e, int x, int y) {
25
26         if (di.isTouching(new Point(x,y))){
27             di.startDrag();
28             return true;
29         }
30         return false;
31     }
32
33     public boolean mouseDrag( Event e, int x, int y) {
34
35         if (di.inMidDrag()) {
36             di.setPosition(new Point(x,y));
37             repaint();
38             return true;
39         }
40         return false;
41     }
42
43     public boolean mouseUp( Event e, int x, int y) {
44
45         if (di.inMidDrag()) {
46             di.endDrag();
47             return true;
48         }
49         return false;
50     }
51
52 }
```

HOW TO DRAG AND DROP IMAGES   135

Listing 2.

```
01 import java.awt.*;
02 import java.awt.image.*;
03
04
05 public class DraggableImage extends Draggable {
06
07     ImageObserver observer;
08     Image image;
09
10     public DraggableImage(ImageObserver o, Image i) {
11         super();    // call Draggable's constructor
12         observer = o;
13         image = i;
14     }
15
16     public boolean isTouching(Point p) {
17
18         return (now.x <= p.x &&
19             p.x <= now.x + image.getWidth(observer) &&
20             now.y <= p.y &&
21             p.y <= now.y + image.getHeight(observer));
22     }
23
24     public void draw (Graphics g, Point p) {
25
26         g.drawImage(image, p.x, p.y, observer);
27     }
28
29 }
```

As the user drags the mouse, the applet's mouseDrag method gets called (lines 33–41). It begins by calling Draggable's inMidDrag in order to detect and ignore click and drags that did not pick up the image. It then passes Draggable's setPosition the new x–y coordinates; setPosition stores the current position in the Point variable then and puts the new position in the Point variable now. After setPosition, the applet calls repaint, which invokes its own paint function.

The applet's paint function invokes Draggable's paint method. Here's where the image is erased at the old position and drawn at the new position. First, paint sets XORMode. Then, since the image is being dragged, paint calls DraggableImage's draw with the old coordinates. With XORMode set, drawing the image in the same place twice erases it. Finally, paint calls draw with the new coordinates, drawing the image at the new location.

136 TECHNIQUES

Listing 3.

```
01  import java.awt.*;
02
03
04  public abstract class Draggable {
05
06      public abstract boolean isTouching(Point p);
07
08      public abstract void draw(Graphics g, Point p);
09
10      Point now, then;
11      boolean being_dragged, drawn;
12
13      public Draggable() {
14          being_dragged = false;
15          now = new Point(0,0);
16          then = new Point(0,0);
17          drawn = true; // don't draw until cooridinates set by client
18      }
19
20      public void startDrag()    { being_dragged = true;}
21      public boolean inMidDrag()          { return being_dragged;}
22      public void  endDrag()        { being_dragged = false; }
23
24      // sync to ensure that now and then remain stable while being drawn
25      public void setPosition(Point p) {
26
27          if (drawn ||// only allow change of coords if already displayed
28          !being_dragged) {  // or if non-dragging (programmatic) change
29
30              then.x = now.x;  // do deep copy
31              then.y = now.y;
32
33              now.x = p.x;
34              now.y = p.y;
35
36              drawn = false;
37          }
38      }
39
40      public void paint( Graphics g, Color c) {
41
42          if (!drawn){
43
44              g.setXORMode(c);
45
46              if (being_dragged)
47              draw(g, then);
48
49              draw(g, now);
50
51              g.setPaintMode();
52
53              drawn = true;
54          }
55      }
56
57  }
```

After returning from the repaint call, mouseDrag exits. This cycle of erasing the image at the old coordinates and drawing it at the new ones continues as long as the user holds the mouse button down and moves the pointer to a new location.

Eventually, mouseUp gets called after the user has dragged the image to the chosen spot and lets go of the button (lines 43–50). mouseUp calls Draggable's endDrag, setting the flag to indicate the user has stopped dragging the image. The image remains at the spot to which it was last dragged.

THE DRAWN FLAG

It's now time to examine the other Boolean flag that Draggable uses, drawn. setPosition and paint use it to prevent setPosition from updating the variables now and then unless paint has already rendered the image at those locations. paint uses drawn to keep from drawing the image twice in the same location inadvertently. Why?

In the first case, setPosition and paint rely upon the drawn flag to combat a thread-related problem. Sometimes the AWT thread's call to applet's paint method gets skipped if the system is busy. If that were to happen while the user was dragging, image fragments would litter the screen. That's because setPosition would update now and then before paint—having been skipped—got a chance to erase image at its old location. The drawn flag prevents this by ensuring that the coordinates are not changed until after the image is moved.

In the second case, paint relies upon the drawn flag to ensure that it only draws an image once. Otherwise, a second call to paint would erase the image, which should only happen if it's being dragged.

POSSIBLE ENHANCEMENTS

So, that's how to implement drag and drop in Java. Various enhancements to this implementation are possible. To track numerous draggables, have the applet put them into a vector and then cycle through them in each spot where it now invokes just one. (See Gamelan's home page for their fun example of drag and drop that uses this style.)

If a large image is used, there will be some flickering as the user drags across the screen. One way to ameliorate the problem is for mouseDrag to call Draggable's paint method directly, instead of calling the applet's repaint method. mouseDrag would need to pass paint the applet's graphics context, which it could get with a call to getGraphics. Double-buffering is another possibility.

Finally, Draggable and DraggableImage could be made multithread safe. This would need to be done if one thread moved the image automatically while another waited for the user to click on it. To do this, put the keyword synchronized before each of the methods in each of the classes (except the constructors) that access the variables now, then, drawn and being_dragged. That would prevent the inconsistent behavior that could arise if one thread were to call a method that changed any of the classes' variables while another thread called a different method that used the same variables.

Jeremy Sevareid is with Random Walk Computing, New York, NY and can be reached by email at jsevareid@randomwalk.com.

URLs

Mr. Potato Head Builder
  http://www.westnet.com/~crywalt/
  pothead/pothead.html

Mr. Potato Head, Java Style
  http://www.westnet.com/~crywalt/
  SpudHead/SpudHead.html

Gamelan's Drag and Drop
  http://www.earthweb.com/java/Throw/

Exception Handling: More Than Just an Add-On Feature

Henry Wong

IN THIS ARTICLE WE review a topic that can be considered very elementary. For many, the time spent trying to understand the exception-handling mechanism for Java is minimal when compared to other areas like multithreading or even interfaces. This is partly due to its similarity to the C++ exception mechanism and to the fact that error handling is still an after-thought in many development shops. (Unfortunately, C++ experience is still a major criteria when hiring Java developers. Hopefully, this will change as Java matures.) In reality, exception handling is more than just an "add-on" feature. When designed properly, it can reduce development time just by not leaving many details that need attention. Furthermore, having exception conditions designed into the framework of the application will make it consistent if not more robust.

We will not examine exception-handling design issues. Those issues are tied closely to the design of the application and can be greatly influenced by the corporate policy that the developer must work under. Instead, we will examine some of the more common details and pitfalls of using exceptions in Java, compare the Java exception mechanism to the C++ exception mechanism, and take a look at exceptions in relation to debugging an application. Hopefully, this look will lead us to better exception-handling designs.

JAVA EXCEPTION PITFALLS

The use of exceptions is very straightforward (See Listing 1). Throwing an exception from a method is similar to returning a result from the

140 Techniques

Listing 1.

```java
public class process {
    private String answer;
    private int error;
    public String Analyze (String data) throws Exception {
        // — process the input —
        switch (error) {
            case 1:
                throw new NullPointerException("Analyzer Failure");
            case 2:
                throw new NumberFormatException("Analyzer Failure");
            default:
                if (error > 0)
                throw new Exception("Unknown Analyzer Failure");
                break;
        }
        return answer;
    }
}

public class engine {
    public static void main (String args[]) throws Exception {
        process p = new process();
        try {
            if (args.length == 1) {
                String result = p.Analyze(args[0]);
            }
        } catch (NullPointerException e) {
            // Handle Null Pointer Exception Here
            throw e;
        } catch (NumberFormatException e) {
            // Handle Number Format Exception Here
        } catch (Exception e) {
            // Handle Generic Exception Here
            throw e;
        }
    }
}
```

method—it is just another type of data that is being returned. This data is of a different type and indicates a result that is different from the traditional return. You might say that this data is an "exception" to the type of data that is returned.

This leads us to a mis-usage of the exception-handling mechanism ("mis-usage" in this case, is based on the opinion of the author, and is formed by having to support many Java and C++ development sites). If an exception is really just data that may be returned, then we should be able to use this mechanism as a way to return many different types of data. Stated in this way, there is nothing wrong with doing this. Issues of

EXCEPTION HANDLING: MORE THAN JUST AN ADD-ON FEATURE   141

performance in execution are merely implementation details—we can assume that they will be fixed in future releases of the JDK. However, this is not a common technique in Java (or even C++) and, while it may make perfect sense to the original developer in an application, it may cause more confusion than it is worth when the application is passed to another developer. It is also much easier to design the method to return a data type that can represent all the possible results. It could be as simple as returning a base class or a new class that can contain the possible return types.

Receiving the exceptions thrown is done by "catching" the exception (See Listing 1). While the traditional way of returning data from the method merely continues the execution, an exception that is thrown from the method will terminate the execution of the "try" block, and continue execution at the "catch" block that matches the exception type. (If no catch block matches the thrown exception, the method that contains the try block will return just as it would have done had it thrown the exception.) These "catch" blocks actually look like mini-methods; depending on what exception is thrown, the thrower can cause the execution of different catch blocks.

This leads us to another mis-usage of exceptions. Exceptions should not be used as a call-back mechanism (i.e., a reverse method call). The confusion caused by using this mechanism does not justify its advantages—especially since there are many more established and efficient techniques of generating call-backs. Even the simple technique of returning a value that can be used to decide which method to call is easier to understand than throwing a call-back exception. Simply reiterated, exceptions should be used to inform the user of error conditions. They should not be used to return a result or to route the execution path of a thread. Applying this simple restriction also makes it easier for the project leader to develop an exception policy for an application (or suite of applications).

A COMPARISON TO C++

For those of us who were originally C++ developers, let's do a comparison of the Java exception-handling mechanism with the C++ exception-handling mechanism. This comparison is from the C++ perception, and would probably concern the C++ developer more than the Java developer. The reason we want to do this is because certain features that are available in C++ are missing in Java. We examine why and how to resolve the

142   Techniques

differences will allow those who are accustomed to C++ exceptions to transfer some of their experience to Java.

The first missing feature in Java noticed by C++ developers is the "rethrow" keyword. This is used in C++ to continue the throwing of an exception after partially handling the exception (See Listing 2). The reason this is necessary is because the catch clause may have "cut-off" part of the exception object. This is caused when the catch clause uses the base class of the exception that is actually thrown. In Java, this is not a problem. Passing of exceptions to the catch clause is always done by reference. This means that while the code in the catch clause is referencing the base class of the object, it is still referring to the original object. To "rethrow" the object, the Java application simply needs to "throw" the object that was originally caught.

Another missing feature in the Java exception-handling mechanism is the ability to catch an object of any type—specified by catching the ellipses in C++ (See Listing 2). Again, this is not necessary in Java. Java does not permit the throwing of primitive types, nor does it allow the throwing of objects that do not derive from the Throwable class. (Java also has a non-enforced policy of only catching exceptions that are derived from the Exception class.) This means that all the objects that can be thrown have the Throwable class as their base class. To catch an object of any type, we simply have to catch the base Throwable class (or the Exception class). Just like C++, Java resolves the catch clause to execute, by checking the catch clauses in order. This means that catching the Exception object should be the last catch clause on the list. Also, if it is desired to throw a primitive type (or an object that does not derive from the Throwable class), we may simply encapsulate the data into a Throwable object.

The last difference with the exception-handling system is a subtle one. Java uses the concept of a finalizer to clean up objects before the object is de-allocated. This is similar to the C++ destructor in that it is also called to clean up the object before the memory is released. The difference is in when it is called. In C++, the destructor is called when the variable goes out of scope or gets deleted. All variables are guaranteed to be destroyed. Even global variables will be destroyed before the application exits. In Java, the finalizer is only called by the garbage collector thread just prior to freeing memory. If the system does not need the memory, the garbage collector will not run; hence the out-of-scope objects will not be finalized. There is also no need to free up memory when an application exits; hence there is no need to finalize objects on exit. (The memory

EXCEPTION HANDLING: MORE THAN JUST AN ADD-ON FEATURE 143

Listing 2.

```
#include <rw/rwstring.h>
#include "exception.h"

class process {
private:
    RWString answer;
    int error;
public:
    process();

    RWString Analyze (RWString data);
};

process::process(void) {}

RWString process::Analyze(RWString data)
{
    // — process the input —
    NullPointerException npe("Analyzer Failure");
    NumberFormatException nfe("Analyzer Failure");
    Exception e("Unknown Analyzer Failure");
    switch (error) {
        case 1:
            throw npe;
        case 2:
            throw nfe;
        default:
            if (error > 0)
            throw e;
            break;
    }
    return answer;
}

int main (int argc, char **argv)
{
    process p;
    try {
        if (argc == 1) {
            RWString result = p.Analyze(argv[0]);
        }
    } catch (NullPointerException e) {
        //Handle Null Pointer Exception Here
        rethrow;
    } catch (NumberFormatException e) {
        //Handle Number Format Exception Here
    } catch (...) {
        //Handle Generic Exception Here
        rethrow;
    }
}
```

144   TECHNIQUES

is actually freed up on exit. It is just done by the OS when the Java virtual machine exits.) Because of this distinction, it is more likely that an application can run out of other resources before it runs out of memory. Depending on the File object's finalizer to close the file will most likely eat up all the system's file handles on a workstation that has a large amount of memory. Of course, the solution is to actively make sure that all the files are closed prior to leaving the scope of the File object.

This is where exceptions may cause a problem. If an exception unrolls the stack, it may cause the method to exit before the file is actively closed. This means that we are now back to depending on the finalizer to free up the resources. To solve this, Java has the concept of a "finally" clause (See Listing 3). The code in the finally clause will always get executed, regardless of whether the try block or the catch block returns, finishes, or throws an exception. It will even get executed if an exception gets thrown past the method. In a way, the finally clause may be thought of as the destructor for the try-catch clause.

EXCEPTIONS, DEBUGGING, AND THREADS

It turns out that there is a stack-trace mechanism that is attached to the exception mechanism. The Throwable class—which all exceptions are

Listing 3.

```java
import java.io.*;

public class Database {
    public boolean process(String filename) throws IOException {
        FileInputStream fis = null;
        try {
            fis = new FileInputStream(filename);
            // Process the file here
            return true;
        } catch (FileNotFoundException fe) {
            fis = null;
            return false;
        } catch (IOException ie) {
            // Just exit here, let the finally
            //  clause close the file.
            throw ie;
        } finally {
            try {
                if (fis != null) fis.close();
            } catch (Exception e) {}
        }
    }
}
```

EXCEPTION HANDLING: MORE THAN JUST AN ADD-ON FEATURE   145

derived from—has two methods that the system uses to inform of any uncaught exceptions. There is a method that will store the current state of the stack and print out the stack trace that is stored. Normally, we do not have to worry about these two methods. When an exception is first instantiated, the state of the stack is stored. And if an exception is thrown so that the entire stack for the executing thread is unrolled, the default exception handler will simply call the method to print the stack trace.

Obviously, we may print out the state of the stack at any time while debugging our application—but there is also a case that we need to be aware of. If we rethrow an exception, we should decide whether the stack information that is stored in the exception object is correct. In Listing 4, the exception handler in the method will rethrow the exception that was generated internally. However, if we do not wish to publish our implementation, there is no need to report the original stack-trace to the caller. In this case, the stack-trace of the current method should be enough debugging information to report that the method generated an error. To accomplish this, the exception handler simply reloads the current stack into the storage area.

The threading system also uses the exception system for internal purposes. When a thread needs to be stopped, the stop() method causes an exception to be thrown from the stopping thread. This causes the stack of the stopping thread to be unrolled. By doing this instead of stopping the thread directly, we can reclaim resources like object locks that are necessary for other threads to function correctly. The actual termination

Listing 4.

```
import java.io.*;

public class Database {
    public boolean process(String filename) throws IOException {
        try {
            // Process the file here !!
            return true;
        } catch (FileNotFoundException fe) {
            return false;
        } catch (IOException ie) {
            // Partially handle the exception and
            // adjust the stack trace here.
            ie.fillInStackTrace();
            throw ie;
        }
    }
}
```

146   Techniques

of the thread is done by the thread itself, upon completion from the run() method. (The run() method can be considered as the main method of a thread.) The reason this works is because there is a policy of not catching any object that does not inherit from the Exception class. The ThreadDeath object that is thrown from the stopping thread inherits from the Error class and hence should not be trapped as the thread stack is unrolled.

This leads us to two more potential pitfalls. (The reason I do not consider these actual pitfalls is because I have not seen any implementation of these techniques and I am unaware of the ramifications of using them.) As mentioned earlier, the policy of not catching any object that does not derive from the exception class is not enforced. This means it is possible to prevent the death of a thread by catching the ThreadDeath object. The thread may then just restart the method that another thread tried to stop. This can be considered a problem because the other thread may be expecting the thread to actually stop, and so may not bother synchronizing data with it.

The other potential pitfall concerns the way the ThreadDeath object is delivered. The stop method is overloaded with a version that specifies the Throwable object that will be used to unroll the stack. This means it is possible to throw an exception for another thread. There are a few problems with using this technique. First, it is unclear just what the other thread is doing at the time of the stop() call. Depending on when the exception is delivered, different results may occur. Second, there is no way for the compiler to check if the exception is actually legal. This means that we can violate the "throws" keyword. While this may be an interesting side-effect of this technique, it may also yield some unexpected results. Finally, the exception that is thrown has the incorrect stack listed in its stack trace. Since the stack is recorded when the throwable object is instantiated, the stack trace is for the calling thread and not the stopping thread. In the case of the ThreadDeath object, this is not a concern because the stack trace is not printed by the default exception handler.

This concludes our assorted look at exceptions. We have tried to define some rules that can help simplify using exceptions within an application, without interfering with other mechanisms related to the exception system, in order to allow us to better design Java applets—using C++ techniques if necessary—by having a better understanding of the error-handling system. Hopefully, this will provide us the tools that will allow us to develop more robust applications.

Tapping the Power of JavaScript

Steven W. Disbrow

WHILE THE JAVA language has been generating the most buzz on the Internet, thousands of HTML authors have been using JavaScript to actually get work done. Although the popularity of JavaScript is growing, the number of ways it is used doesn't seem to be. During my travels on the Web, I've noticed that people seem to believe that JavaScript is only good for creating those "crawling" announcements in the status line of the browser or for creating a clock that tells you the time. While these are fine uses for mom and pop pages on the Internet, they don't take advantage of everything that JavaScript can do and certainly don't have much use on corporate intranets.

I will demonstrate how to go beyond these uses of JavaScript and how to manipulate data that results from a live database query. *(Note: The examples in this article assume you are using Microsoft's Internet Information Server version 1.0 or later. However, the concepts [and JavaScript code] should easily translate to other Internet server platforms.)*

THE PROBLEM

If your Web site is anything like mine, you probably have several databases that just sit around waiting for user queries. In most cases, these queries are dull, simple things that require you to pull one or more fields from the database and return them to the user unchanged. But, once the boss sees those simple reports on his/her monitor, he/she's likely to ask for some that are more complex, and that's where the trouble starts.

For example, consider an apparently simple report where you have to show a running total created from a set of numbers that are stored in a database (see Table 1). (In this example, it's a Microsoft Access database,

148   TECHNIQUES

Table 1.   Report showing a running total.

Product	Sold This Qtr	Sold For	Total This Item	Running Total
Booster	2	$ 8	$ 16	$ 16
Betsy Wetsy	99	$ 20	$ 1,980	$ 1,996
TurboDude	500	$ 10	$ 5,000	$ 6,996
Teen Barbara	1,000	$ 15	$15,000	$ 21,996

but it can be any type of database that your Web server will let you link to.) Because we are using Internet Information Server for this example, there are two ways we can link to our database: the Internet Database Connector (IDC) or Microsoft's dbWeb. (Note that IDC is included with Internet Information Server and dbWeb is available for free from Microsoft's Web site. If you haven't done so already, be sure to read the IDC documentation after you finish this article.)

IDC is a low-level protocol that lets you connect to any Open Database Connectivity (ODBC) compliant database and extract information from it based on an SQL query string. (See Listing 1 for the IDC file.) dbWeb is more of a high-level "wizard" for connecting to ODBC databases. Instead of writing your queries (and the necessary SQL statements) by hand, you fill in a series of dialog boxes with information and the dbWeb application generates the necessary SQL. Besides being easier to use, another advantage of dbWeb over IDC is that it allows you to access the custom queries that you have saved with your database. So, if your database has a complex query already saved in it, dbWeb can actually run that query for you and plug any of the results into the HTML page you send back to the user.

You may be wondering, "Why do we need JavaScript for this stuff?" The answer lies in this example. (It's a bit contrived, but it's also a real-world example.) When you use Access, there are only two ways (that I've found) to create a running total in a database. The first is to create an Access report and save it with the file. This is a great solution, except that neither IDC nor dbWeb will let you extract data from an Access report. The second is to create an Access database query and use VisualBASIC for Applications (VBA) to create a function that generates a running total inside that query. The catch here is that IDC doesn't allow you to pull data from a saved Access query and dbWeb doesn't allow you to pull data from an Access query that calls a Visual BASIC function!

(Note that there *are* two other ways to create this type of report on the Web via Access. The first uses Microsoft's Internet Assistant for Access

TAPPING THE POWER OF JAVASCRIPT   149

```
Listing 1. simple.idc links ODBC data to simple.htx

Datasource: Simple
Username: admin
Template:c:\webshare\wwwroot\jstest\simple.htx
SQLStatement:
 +SELECT simple.product,
 +simple.price,
 +simple.numsold
 +FROM simple
 +ORDER by VAL(simple.numsold);
```

to generate an HTML version of the appropriate Access report. The second creates a new database that contains our running total and queries that database instead. Neither solution is satisfactory because the reports wouldn't be automatically updated when and if the original data changed. We want something that will rebuild our report on demand from the latest available data.)

THE SOLUTION

This brings us back to JavaScript. Because we can't get the data into a format we need on the server side of the query, the next best solution is to take the raw data returned from the query and use JavaScript to create the report we want inside the client's browser.

To do this, we must create a JavaScript object that both computes and reports on our running total. And because this is a business report, it might not be a bad idea to take the time to format our numbers as dollar values with commas in all the appropriate places.

Near the top of Listing 2 you'll see the basic JavaScript object we'll use for this task (the runSum object) as well as the two methods (getSum and addToSum) that we'll use to access the fields in the object. Following that is the code that formats a number as a dollar amount. Even if you aren't a professional programmer, this code should look fairly simple. The tricky part is using this code with IDC or dbWeb to generate the report we want.

THE TRICKY PART

When you use IDC or dbWeb to generate a report, you not only specify an ODBC database to query (specified on the line that begins with "Datasource:" in Listing 1), you also specify a special template file (with the

Listing 2. The simple.htx report template file

```html
<HTML>
<HEAD>
<TITLE>Report - Simple RunningTotal</TITLE>
<SCRIPT LANGUAGE="JAVASCRIPT">
/* The runSum object encapsulates our running sum */
/* This particular function sets up a new runSum */
/* object and sets its initial total to the value */
/* specified by startTotal.           */
function runSum( startTotal) {
    /* initialize the total */
    this.total =startTotal;

    /* set up the other methods for this object */
    this.getSum =getSum;
    this.addToSum =addToSum;
    }

/* This method returns the current total from a runSum object */
function getSum() {
    return this.total;
    }

/* This method adds to the current total of a runSum object */
function addToSum(theValue) {
    this.total =this.total + theValue;
    }

/* Set up our running sum for this report */
theSum = new runSum( 0);

/* This function adds commas to a numeric string */
function addCommas( theValue) {
    var tempStr = "+ theValue;
    var finalStr =";
    var theLen =tempStr.length;
    var index;
    var groupCount =0;

    /* Check for a decimal place */
    if(tempStr.indexOf('.') == -1)
        index =theLen - 1;
    else {
        index =tempStr.indexOf('.') - 1;
        finalStr =tempStr.substring(index + 1, theLen);
        }

    /* Check for a value less than 1,000 */
    if (theLen <=3){
        finalStr =tempStr;
        }
    else {
        /* Move back through the string, breaking */
        /* off groups of 3 digits          */
        while(index >= 0) {
            finalStr = tempStr.charAt(index) + finalStr;
            groupCount = groupCount + 1;
            if(groupCount == 3) {
                (index != 0) {
                    finalStr = ',' + finalStr;
                    }
                groupCount = 0;
                }
            index= index - 1;
            }
        }

    return finalStr;
    }

/* This function converts a value into a dollar string with commas
and the like */
function toDollars( theValue) {
    return '$' +addCommas( theValue);
    }
</SCRIPT>
```

```html
</HEAD>
<BODY BGCOLOR="WHITE">
<H1><CENTER>QueryResults</CENTER></H1>
<P>
<CENTER>
<FONT SIZE=-1>

<TABLE>
<!-- The report titles -->
<TR>
<TD><FONTSIZE=-1><B><U>Product</U></B></FONT></TD>
<TD><FONT SIZE=-1><B><U>Sold ThisQuarter</B></U></FONT></TD>
<TD><FONT SIZE=-1><B><U>SoldFor</U></B></FONT></TD>
<TD><FONT SIZE=-1><B><U>Total ThisItem</U></B></FONT></TD>
<TD><FONT SIZE=-1><B><U>RunningTotal</U></B></FONT></TD>
</TR>

<!-- Detail row. A new row will be included for each record returned
from the query -->
<%begindetail%>
<TR>
<TD><FONTSIZE=-1><%Product%></FONT></TD>

<!-- Use JavaScript to put commas in our number of units sold -->
<TD><FONT SIZE=-1>
<SCRIPT language="javascript">
document.write( addCommas(<%numsold%>));
</SCRIPT>
</FONT>
</TD>

<!-- Use JavaScript to convert the price to a dollar amount -->
<TD><FONT SIZE=-1>
<SCRIPT LANGUAGE="JAVASCRIPT">
document.write( toDollars(<%price%>));
</SCRIPT>
</FONT>
</TD>

<!-- Use JavaScript to compute the sales total for this item and
convert that to a dollar amount -->
<TD><FONT SIZE=-1>
<SCRIPT LANGUAGE="JAVASCRIPT">
document.write( toDollars( <%price%>* <%numsold%>));
</SCRIPT>
</FONT>
</TD>

<!-- Use JavaScript to update our running total and to print it out as
a dollar amount -->
<TD><FONT SIZE=-1>
<SCRIPT LANGUAGE="JAVASCRIPT">
theSum.addToSum( <%price%> *<%numsold%>);
document.write( toDollars(theSum.getSum()));
</SCRIPT>
</FONT>
</TD>

</TR>
<%enddetail%>
<!-- End of Detail Row -->
</TABLE>
<HR>

<%if CurrentRecord EQ 0%>
<BR>
<P>
<I>No matching records were found.</I><P>
<%endif%>
</CENTER>
</FONT>
</BODY>
</HTML>
```

TAPPING THE POWER OF JAVASCRIPT   151

file type .htx) that IDC or dbWeb will use to generate the final HTML code that gets sent back to the browser (specified on the line that begins with "Template:" in Listing 1). This file is an HTML "skeleton" that defines the basic HTML of the resulting report, as well as the database fields that are to be merged into the report (Listing 2).

Listing 2 has several init strings that look like this: <%variablename%>. (Listing 2, intended for use with IDC. dbWeb, is almost exactly the same with a few minor syntax differences.) These tag strings mark the places where the fields returned from the ODBC database will be merged with the contents of the template file to create the final HTML output. The string <%product%> marks where the contents of the database's "product" field will be inserted into the final HTML that is sent to the browser.

That's simple enough, but the real power of the IDC/dbWeb/JavaScript combination is unleashed by placing JavaScript commands between the <%begindetail%> and <%enddetail%> tags. These IDC tags (and their dbWeb equivalents) don't represent any one database field. Instead, they specify that for every database record that comes back from the query, the HTML (and JavaScript) code between these tags should be *repeated* in the final HTML file that is sent back to the browser. By placing JavaScript commands inside these tags, we can execute those JavaScript commands *for each record* that is returned by the query!

This record-level access means that, for each record we get back, we can (as shown in Table 1):

1. Display a product name.
2. Display a quantity sold (with any necessary commas inserted by a JavaScript function).
3. Display the amount it was sold for (converted to a dollar amount via a JavaScript function).
4. Display the total sales for this item (also as a dollar amount).
5. Update our running sum of all the sales amounts.
6. Display that running sum (as another dollar amount).

The great thing is that only the first three fields we display (product name, quantity, and unit price) actually came from our database. (See Table 2 for the structure of our sample database.) The rest were computed on the fly by our JavaScript functions using the data from the records that were returned by the query.

152 Techniques

Table 2. Structure of our sample database.

Name	Field Type
product	text
price	text
numsold	text

If this seems mind-numbingly simple, it is! But, it's also *very* powerful. I've used this same technique to create on-the-fly charts (by using JavaScript to call a Java charting applet) based on query results, and to create dynamic links to other sites that were relevant to the results of the query. These features are simple enough to create using this technique but allow your Web site much more flexibility.

GOTCHAS

Even though this is a simple technique, there are a few pitfalls to watch out for. The first is that when you work with ODBC, different ODBC drivers will treat the same types of data slightly differently. For example, when I switched from the Access 6 ODBC driver to the Access 7 ODBC driver, the dollar signs that I had been getting back from my database were suddenly gone. Because I had been stripping these off (to perform calculations in JavaScript), I had to make some changes to my JavaScript code to compensate for the change. So, the JavaScript code you write for one ODBC driver may not work exactly the same with the next one you use.

Second, you must be sure that you're aware of what type of data is coming back from your database. Generally speaking, JavaScript won't care what the type is (it will do the appropriate conversion automatically), but the other tools you use (like ODBC) might care a great deal! Notice that the ORDER BY clause in Listing 1 converts the numsold field into a numeric value. If this wasn't done, the report wouldn't be sorted properly. Why? Well, if you look at Table 2, you'll notice that all the fields are defined as "text" fields; even the fields (like the numsold field) that would be better defined as numbers. If you think this is a silly thing to do, I agree. However, I did it that way because almost every "legacy" database that I've had to work with on the Web has been designed this way. So, check that database structure before you begin designing your queries and reports and don't assume anything!

TAPPING THE POWER OF JAVASCRIPT 153

```
Listing 3. HTML query via IDC.
<html>

<head>
<title>Simple Query</title>
</head>

<body bgcolor="white">
<h1>Query Test Page</h1>
<p> </p>
<formaction="http://www.yoursite.com/scripts/
  simple.idc?" method="GET">
<p>
<input type=submit name="RunQuery" value="Run Query">
</p>
</form>
</body>

</html>
```

Finally, while I've discussed both IDC and dbWeb throughout this article, I need to point out that after several months of experimentation, I've concluded that using dbWeb should be avoided if at all possible. While I'm sure Microsoft will fix dbWeb soon, I've found that version 1.x of dbWeb tends to hang after handling a fairly small number of queries. IDC, on the other hand, while a bit harder to learn, appears to be rock solid and able to handle any number of queries.

CONCLUSION

I hope I have convinced you that JavaScript can be used for something other than just scrolling text and telling time. By combining JavaScript with other Web tools at your disposal, and using these combinations to manipulate the actual *data* on your Web pages, you can create content that you wouldn't otherwise be able to create. If you come up with a cool new use for this technique be sure to let me know!

Steven Disbrow is the owner of EGO Systems, Hixson, TN. He is a freelance programmer and writer. He can be contacted at diz@chattanooga.net.

```
URL
Microsoft Corporation
  http://www.microsoft.com
```

SECTION SEVEN

DISTRIBUTED COMPUTING

Distributed Business Applications Using Java: An Implementation Framework

Radha Bandarpalle and Raj Ratnakar

ONE OF THE PRIMARY drivers for enterprise computing is to support corporate business functions in a dynamic, complex, and competitive environment. Java programming language and development environment is a tool that can help businesses increase customers' access to new products and services. This article discusses evolutionary stages of interactions between Enterprise Information Systems (EIS) and customers. We propose an implementation framework for the development of business applications in a distributed object computing (DOC) environment using Java.

INTRODUCTION

The globalization of customer base and markets has put the onus on businesses to distribute marketing efforts to extend their reach. In their endeavor to reduce cycle time from product innovation to delivery to service, businesses have recognized information systems as a key partner. New techniques, architectural frameworks, and programming languages are constantly emerging and are proving to be evolutionary steps that assist businesses in coping with the marketing revolution. Java, a programming language, in conjunction with distributed object computing and existing enterprise client/server applications, can help businesses reduce cycle time and increase their market reach and productivity.

158   DISTRIBUTED COMPUTING

EVOLUTION OF DISTRIBUTED BUSINESS APPLICATIONS

An enterprise information model consists of several business applications; the precise number depends on the nature and the size of the business. These interacting business applications must interface with database(s) for data storage and retrieval, and must provide an access mechanism to the customer. To reach a large customer base, businesses are providing innovative access methods that evolve continually. A majority of these changes have eliminated drawbacks and have added functionality to the existing techniques. We discuss three evolutionary stages (see Fig. 1) of methods and techniques by which customers can have access to the services and products of an enterprise.

Stage 1: In this stage, customers can place an order through e-mail, phone, or mail. This technique is most widely used because organizations can reach a very broad customer base. The major drawbacks of such a system are:

- Complexity in handling large volumes.
- Static interfaces.
- Costly and error-prone human interface.

Stage 2: This stage was characterized by the PC revolution and the increased use of the Internet. It prompted a number of enterprises to offer custom software to customers to help them access business services via direct modem or the Internet, in addition to e-mail, phone, and mail orders. The major drawbacks of this technique are:

- Difficulty in delivering software upgrades to customers with changes in product offerings.
- Platform dependence resulting in multiple development efforts.

Stage 3: The developments in Internet browser technology and the use of HTML forms and CGI scripts further encouraged enterprises to bring their products and services closer to customers. Businesses can offer their services by setting up HTML/CGI-based pages and software on their servers and advertising the URL addresses, thus eliminating the need for distribution of software. However, this approach still has the following major drawbacks:

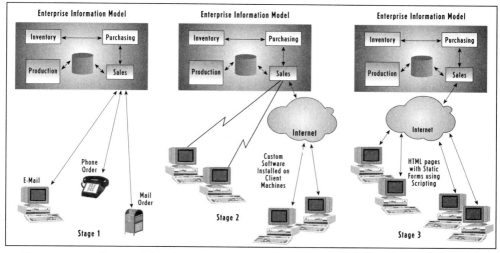

Figure 1. Evolution of distributed business applications.

- Static interfaces.
- Poor performance.
- Lack of interoperability with current client/server architectures.
- Lack of scalability (it is difficult to achieve load-balancing during peak access).
- Inability to dynamically transfer requests for business services between servers.

Typically organizations such as airlines, banking and financial investment companies, retail stores, etc., will find their business applications in one of the above stages of evolution. The need to migrate from one stage to another depends on customer profiles of individual organizations.

ROLE OF JAVA IN DISTRIBUTED BUSINESS APPLICATIONS

As the previous section points out, service offerings by businesses using HTML-based static forms and CGI scripts have numerous limitations. Java, a "portable, interpreted, high-performance, simple, object-oriented" programming language (*The Java Language Environment,* a white paper from Sun Microsystems, October 1995), provides a means for downloading dynamic and intelligent GUI/OOUI applications as Java applets

160   DISTRIBUTED COMPUTING

embedded in the HTML pages. These applets can then run efficiently on client machines that support the Java runtime environment. The applets can be standalone, such as a simple spreadsheet, or can be distributed, such as a user interface for an airline-reservation system, which provides complex client/server interaction. The capabilities of client/server Java applets make it a strong contender for use in distributed business applications development.

Potentially, ideal candidates for distributing their business applications using Java are likely to have the following characteristics:

- Large, geographically distributed customer base.
- High frequency of customer and business function interaction.
- Customer accessibility to Internet services.
- Transaction-oriented business functions.

The client application developed using Java is downloaded as an applet that encapsulates the business process. Customers can access the pages for the business, based on known URLs (see Fig. 2). The application can then offer a number of business services. The application can accept commands, gather requirements, and communicate with the server to provide business services requested by the client. The click of a button invokes a client application's GUI. The interface offers facilities to make queries. For example, in an airline-reservation system, a query for all the fares between two cities brings back a result set containing quotes on different airlines with associated restrictions. The customer can then, with the click of a menu-button, perform sorts, apply filters, and evaluate options, without querying the server again. This makes the GUI more user-friendly and responsive. Information systems in other such businesses can similarly harness the capabilities of Java to improve customer interactions in their business processes.

IMPLEMENTATION FRAMEWORK

Numerous architectural and implementation frameworks for distributed client/server applications have evolved in the past few years. The most widely used three-tier client/server model (see *Client/Server Architectures*, a white paper by Clarke, Bowman, and Stikeleather, Technical Resource Connection, 1995) is comprised of three components: client process that maintains presentation logic, server process that holds the data manage-

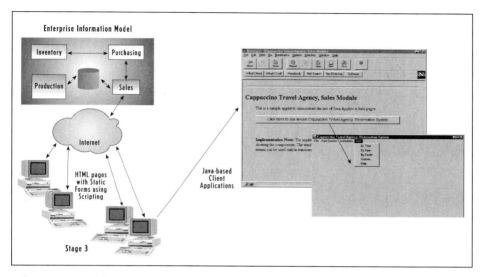

Figure 2. Java-based distributed business application implementation.

ment logic, and the middle tier, which contains business application logic and transport. However, as Orfali, Harkey, and Edwards point out in *The Essential Distributed Objects Survival Guide* (Wiley, 1996), the current client/server implementations are difficult to develop and maintain, besides resulting in multiple monolithic applications. In recent years, advances in the use of object-oriented technology and in the evolution of distributed object computing have rendered the concept of monolithic applications archaic.

The Object Management Group's (OMG) Object Management Architecture (OMA) and its CORBA specifications have emerged as *de facto* industry standards for distribution of objects. We discuss two implementation frameworks for distributed business applications using Java. The socket-based solution for communication between Java client and the server can be used in both the aforementioned architectures. The ORB-based implementation model is specific to OMA.

SOCKET-BASED CLIENT/SERVER INTERACTION

Figure 3 illustrates how Java client application(s) and enterprise server(s) communicate using socket interfaces. The socket classes provided by Java encapsulate creation, connection establishment/acceptance, read/write (using stream objects), and error-handling. Extension of these classes to

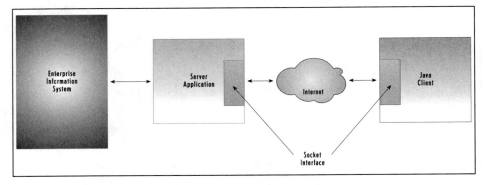

Figure 3. Socket-based client/server interaction.

address application-related communication needs would further simplify implementation of interactive business services. However, this framework will still have to contend with inherent disadvantages (see "Comparing Alternate Client-Side Distributed Programming Techniques," Schmidt and Vinoski, *C++ Report,* May 1995) of sockets and streams such as increased code complexity and overhead associated with implementation and maintenance of message-parsing schema.

CORBA-BASED IMPLEMENTATION FRAMEWORK

A CORBA-based implementation overcomes the limitations of sockets. An ORB is "a mechanism that lets objects transparently make requests to—and receive responses from—other objects located locally or remotely" (from Orfali, Harkey, and Edwards' *The Essential Distributed Objects Survival Guide,* Wiley, 1996). It is responsible for finding the object implementation for the request (service location), preparing the object implementation to receive the request (service invocation), and communicating the data making up the request (parameters passing) (see *The Common Object Request Broker: Architecture and Specification,* Revision 2.0, Object Management Group, July 1995). Client applications using Java can use the ORB for direct invocation of object services offered by business process objects residing on enterprise servers. The ORB can be extended via Internet to the client machines without any requirement for the vendor-specific ORB software. The CORBA-client functionality needed to utilize the ORB services is downloaded along with the Java applet as embedded

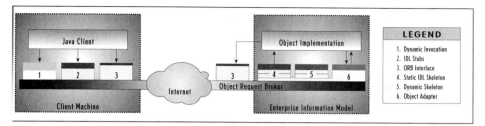

Figure 4. CORBA-based client/server interaction.

imports. Figure 4 relates the CORBA architecture to this implementation framework.

The Java client software can interface with the business service objects in one of two ways. It can use OMG's Interface Definition Language (IDL) stubs generated by the use of an IDL-Java compiler, in which case the interfaces would be statically bound during compile time. It can also make use of the Dynamic Invocation Interfaces (DII), which provide a mechanism by which the interfaces to business service objects are discovered and invoked at run time. This, however, would require business service objects to register their interfaces with an Interface Repository service, as defined in CORBA 2.0. In either of these two approaches, the client objects would be free from dealing with the communication issues between the client and the server.

In addition to benefits derived from compliance with industry standards, business applications developed using Java client objects in a CORBA framework stand to reap the following benefits:

- Transparency to low-level communication interfaces.
- Truly distributed client objects interacting with OMA services such as naming, persistence, transaction, query, etc.
- Language independence between client and server object implementations.
- Polymorphic messaging ability between client and server objects.

SO, WHAT DOES JAVA BUY US?

With the continuing PC revolution and increasing use of Internet services by businesses to extend their customer reach, tools such as the Java programming language will gain importance. Combined with distributed

164 Distributed Computing

object computing, Java will help enterprises realize their business needs. Specifically, client applications that interface with enterprise information systems can harness the following characteristics of Java:

- A dynamic user interface characterized by menus, pop-up menus, context-sensitive help, etc.
- Client applications with embedded intelligence that enhance presentations such as sort, filter, etc.
- Reduced development costs because of platform independence.
- Reduced deployment and maintenance efforts because of real-time software download on demand.

As ORBs evolve to provide mappings for Java, IDEs automate Java development, and object databases support Java objects, the use of this technology for business applications development will become ubiquitous.

Radha Bandarpalle is an Information Architect and Raj Ratnakar an OO-Modeler with The Technical Resource Connection, Tampa, FL. The authors can be reached at radha@trcinc.com or ratnakar@trcinc.com.

The Java.net Library

Adam Freeman and Darrel Ince

THE JAVA.NET PACKAGE allows developers to create and manage network connections. We explain how to build a server and demonstrate that the same principles can be used to create functional clients. We focus on the package and not on the "back-end" functionality that would tailor the code to specific applications. We feel that the network package is one of the most flexible and important elements of the Java system, and we fully expect to see it become an essential tool in Java development—especially in applet development. Using the network classes enables a Java applet to reach out beyond the confines of the Web browser and create an environment where the user can access information in a coordinated model, restricted only by the user's capacity to absorb data.

THE COMMON PROTOCOL

One criticism of the network support within the Java package libraries is that TCP/IP is the only protocol that is not always available as part of the standard operating system software in non-UNIX environments.

While some platforms have better support for other protocols, the selection of IP for the Java libraries is reasonable given that it is the *de facto* protocol for the Internet and has been ported to a whole range of platforms. Additionally, supporting a range of protocols that are not uniformly available on all platforms that can run Java would inhibit the intrinsic cross-platform nature of the Java language and limit the cross-connectivity that makes Java such a useful language.

However, there are bound to be problems that require Java and the use of a protocol other than TCP/IP. In these cases all is not lost: it is possible, albeit challenging, to write methods that implement other protocols. By using native methods it is also possible to take advantage of existing

165

166   DISTRIBUTED COMPUTING

system libraries to manage network connections. While it is possible to create such support for your Java applications, our advice is to stick with the TCP/IP support within the standard Java libraries wherever possible; this level of support will be sufficient for the majority of development efforts.

WRITING A SERVER

We'll start our descriptions of client/server functionality with the server end of things. Our goal will be to write a simple server that will accept network connections and then write back any strings that the client sends in. It's a simple goal. However, it serves as an excellent way of introducing the libraries. For the reader impatient to see big applications, we would advise you to imagine that instead of simply returning a string, the server carries out some major set of functions such as accessing a huge database, making several complex and involved queries, and then returning the string.

THE COST OF USING JAVA FOR SERVERS

Java is not always the best language for writing servers. One of the biggest problems is the delay that is incurred while the Java runtime software loads and interprets the Java code. This means that if a server crashes and then is restarted, there is a significant delay before service is restored. This is not always a problem. However, if high availability and fast response are important to your application, then Java may not be the best of choices. This may not be a problem when full compilers are available for Java, but currently, it presents a challenge to developers.

Of course, there is a cost in not using Java as the server. The development team must write in different languages with potentially different approaches to networking. Java has an excellent network library that may not be matched in other languages, and since Java is cross-platform, it is possible to deploy the server software on a range of platforms—a feature that should not be underestimated.

INTRODUCING THE FIRST ITERATION
OF THE SERVER

This first version of the server will just wait for a connection and then write the string received from the connection to the out channel of the

THE JAVA.NET LIBRARY   167

server process. When the string has been printed out, the application will quit. As a rule, it is only possible to have servers running as part of Java applications because of the security constraints imposed on applet code by the Web browser that embeds the Java runtime system.

The code for the server is shown in Listing 1.

If we compile this file and run the server, we can then telnet into port 6001 and type a string. The string is printed out on the server output and then the server exits. It is worth walking through the code to explain what is happening. The first class, server1, just contains the main() method that all applications have to implement. The class creates a new instance of simpleServer and passes the port we wish to use as an argument. All of the work happens in the simpleServer class. Looking at the constructor, we can see that the first line of code is

```
sock = new ServerSocket(port);
```

This creates a new ServerSocket called sock. What is a socket? Well, without going into much detail, a socket is a combination of a host and a port. A host is a (possibly) remote computer that supports the TCP/IP protocol and a port is the part of the computer that you talk to for a given service. So certain ports are used for sending e-mail, starting terminal sessions and even playing games. You can think of a port as a way of telling the computer which software or service you would like to use.

The ServerSocket creates a network connection on the machine that is prepared to accept connections from client machines in order to provide some kind of service. The number that is passed as an argument specifies which port we want to use. In order to let clients access our simple service the client software must have some prior knowledge of the port number that we are using. Well-known services have a set of ports that are universally recognized; ports that have a number less than 1024 are considered "special" on many implementations of TCP/IP and require system privileges to be used. The danger in selecting a port at random is that if your software is later moved to another server, it is possible that another piece of network software is already expecting to use the port that you have selected and your software will die reporting that the port is in use.

The best way of dealing with this is to provide a mechanism for allowing the user to specify an alternative port on the command line that can override the default that the software uses. At the moment, we have created the socket connection for the server but nothing else will happen.

Listing 1.

```java
import java.lang.*;
import java.net.*;
import java.util.*;
import java.io.*;

public class server1 {
    public static void main(String args[]) {
    /* Create a new instance of the simpleServer */
    simpleServer ss = new simpleServer(6001);
    }
}

class simpleServer {
    ServerSocket sock;
    Socket conn;
    BufferedInputStream instream;
    String str;

    simpleServer(int port) {
        try {
            /* Try to be a server on this port */
            sock = new ServerSocket(port);
            System.out.println("Started on port " + port);
            conn = sock.accept();
        } catch(Exception e) {
            System.out.println("Err: " + e);
            System.exit(1);
        }

        try {
            /* Create the stream to the socket */
            instream = new
            BufferedInputStream(conn.getInputStream());
        } catch(Exception e) {
            System.out.println("Err: " + e);
            System.exit(1);
        }
        /* Read line from the socket and then
        write it out */
        str = this.getline();
        System.out.println("Str: " + str.trim());
    }

    public String getline() {
        StringBuffer strbuf = new StringBuffer();
        int tmp;
            do {
            try {
                /* Try to read from the stream */
                tmp = instream.read();
            } catch(Exception e) {
            return(null);
            }
            if (tmp == -1) {
                /* There is nothing to read */
                return(null);
            }
            if (tmp != 0) {
                /* Add character to StringBuffer */
                strbuf.append((char)tmp);
            }
            } while (tmp != '\n');
                /* Return the String of the StringBuffer */
                return(strbuf.toString());
        }
    }
}
```

THE JAVA.NET LIBRARY   169

We need to tell the socket that it should accept a connection when one arrives. This is done with the call

```
conn = sock.accept();
```

This tells the ServerSocket that it should wait for a connection. Because it is impossible to predict when a connection request will arrive from a client, making the call blocks the thread of execution until a connection is made to the port. Until this happens, no other lines of code are processed. (This is fine when the server is expected to cope with only one client, but if there are multiple clients, having the entire execution halted until another client arrives is not workable.) Notice that the call to accept() is grouped with the ServerSocket call, so that if there are problems establishing the port, the code doesn't send a message to an object that could not be created. If there are problems in establishing the ServerSocket, then the error is printed to the out channel and the application exits by means of the code:

```
System.exit(1)
```

The argument 1 to the call of exit enables the system to provide an error code that gives an indication of the problem.

The next few lines of code create the required streams to let us read from the socket. When these lines of Java are executed, we already have a connection established from a client. We know this because the call to accept() blocks execution until this is true. In this example, we have chosen to use a BufferedInputStream from the java.iopackage. We have to catch the exceptions because the call could generate a problem. The alternative would be to declare that our class can throw the same exception, but this approach has the cost of losing the resolution that is provided by catching exceptions at the point in the code where they are thrown.

If the application has successfully created the ServerSocket, accepted an incoming connection request and dealt with the I/O streams, we can then read a line of input from the socket connection. This line of input will be the line that the user has typed. We have defined a separate method called getline() to handle this task. In essence, getline() reads a byte from the stream we have associated with the socket (it is not possible to read and write directly to sockets—instead, you must associate a stream using the getInputStream() and getOutputStream() methods). If the byte is equal to −1 then there is no input from the user waiting to be read. If the byte is not equal to 0, then we make a cast from the integer value of the byte

170 DISTRIBUTED COMPUTING

to a char and place the character into a StringBuffer. When the character matches \n (which is the code for the return key) we send back the String representation of the StringBuffer. At this point, simpleServer prints out the line that getline() returned, and since there are no other lines of code to execute, the application exits.

OTHER TASKS WITH SOCKETS

So far we have shown you how to build a basic server. When deploying the server code in your own projects, there are hooks to handle the application-specific processing as required. In this section we will look at some of the other methods that are related to sockets.

IDENTIFYING THE CLIENT

While some servers will be available to the whole of the Internet, others may contain information or services that could be restricted to clients from particular sites or from a certain list. The socket class provides a mechanism for obtaining the address of the client to which it is connected.

Here is a code fragment that illustrates how to get the IP address of a client:

```
...
ServerSocket ss = new ServerSocket(3000);
Socket sock = ss.accept();
InetAddress addr = sock.getInetAddress();
System.out.println("Address: " +
                    addr.toString());
...
```

This code creates a ServerSocket that is listening to port 3000 (for brevity we have omitted the exception handling that is required) and then accept() is called that will block the thread of execution until a client connects to the port. When a connection is made, the socket is created and then we make a call to getInetAddress(), which returns the address in the form of an InetAddress. We convert the address to a String and then print it out. Instead of just printing it, we could have put some further processing in—for example, to make a comparison to check that the address matches a predefined set of rules.

THE INETADDRESS

This is the first time that we have used the InetAddress and it is sufficiently useful to be worthy of some discussion. The InetAddress is an object that is related to an IP address; it can be thought of as the call-sign that computers using TCP/IP will use to identify themselves. Like call-signs, IP addresses can be changed (within some constraints that are beyond the scope of this article), and therefore it is worth remembering that checking that the IP address of the client matches an address in the ruleset is not a guarantee that everything is fine. However, for simple security and usage logging, getting the IP address from the socket is sufficient.

So what can you do with an IP address? IP addresses are typically associated with hostnames. For example, the address 206.26.48.100 is associated with the machine called "java.sun.com." The network package provides support for looking up names based on numbers and numbers based on names. Here is a simple code fragment to illustrate the point:

```
...
ServerSocket ss = newServerSocket(3000);
Socket sock = ss.accept();
InetAddress addr = sock.getInetAddress();
System.out.println("Address: " +
                    addr.getHostName());
...
```

This is very similar to the previous fragment, with the exception that when we print out the line of information we make a call to the getHostName() method; this returns a String containing the name. This is more useful for screening hosts than working with "raw" IP numbers. For example, if we only wanted to allow access from hosts that are part of the Sun network, we could look for hostnames that end with "sun.com" or "sun.co.uk" instead of having to maintain a list of the network ranges that Sun uses.

It is worth noting that the call to getHostName() returns the name that was returned from the local name services implemented on your machine. For example, if the code was executed on a Sun, then the name returned to the call will vary depending on whether the information came from the local files, the NIS service or the DNS. Equally possible is the chance that the client has not been registered in the name services properly and

172 DISTRIBUTED COMPUTING

so there is no entry available at all. When basing code decisions on something as potentially variable as hostnames, it is advisable to make sure that the information that is returned from the call is the information that you are expecting, especially if granting access has some financial or security implications.

It is also possible to perform the operation in reverse, taking the name of a machine and obtaining the IP address. This is done through the getByName() and getAllByName() methods that return the addresses associated with a hostname. The getAllByName() method returns all of the IP addresses that a machine has registered; typically, this is applicable to large server machines that require multiple network connections for increased speed or robustness of service.

One other useful method that is associated with InetAddress is getLocalHost(), which returns the IP address of the local machine. This is useful for all sorts of applications, not least of which is having a network client report the IP address of the machine it is using for logging purposes.

WRITING AN APPLET

The previous section covered the use of the network package to develop a server process for a Java application. Java also supports network access for applets. In this section we will illustrate the use of the network package within applets.

Applet Security

Network access from applets is subject to some constraints. The most significant limitation is that applets can only make network connections to the host that they were downloaded from. This constraint is imposed by a Web browser that operates a strict security policy. Each browser is allowed to implement a different security model or to allow the user to switch between models; at the time of writing, the browser that is most likely to have the majority of users, Netscape Navigator, will implement a heavily constrained model that is not modifiable by the user.

There have been some releases of code that allow the developer to bypass the security model by taking control of network connections that were intended for other purposes and were therefore not subject to the same constraints as applet socket connections. While these approaches may work, we would advise against using them for two reasons. First, such security loopholes are likely to be addressed as Java products become more stable and may make your code break in later releases of the system. Second, subverting other connections without the express knowledge of the user violates any trust that the user has in the software. Applet developers are constrained within a tightly controlled environment, and violating the rules undermines user confidence in the applet and in Java as a whole.

Our First Look at a Client

A simple example of a client will be described in this section. This client will connect to a port and then print out whatever output the server produces. This is not very useful for interactive services such as telnet telnet or ftp but does work with the daytime service that simply prints out the current time and exits. Our code will make a socket connection to the server and then read back a line of output that will be printed to the standard channel out. Listing 2 shows the code for it.

If you have read the preceding section, this code should make sense to you. The arguments are used to supply a hostname and a port to connect to. For example, to access the day/time server on the local UNIX machine, it would be possible to type

```
java simpleClient localhost 13
```

and the output would be the date and time. Because the arguments are expected to be a String and an integer representing the hostname and the port, using the names of the service will not work. For example:

```
java simpleClient localhost daytime
```

would not work because the call to Integer.parseInt() would generate an exception and the default settings would be used. If this were a real-world application and not an example, it would be a good idea to give the user some indication that the arguments that have been supplied have failed and the defaults are being used. If this is not done, the user could make any kind of mistake and not notice that the software has defaulted to other parameters.

Once the arguments have been processed, we create a new instance of a class called simpleHandler that will do all of the work. The first thing that simpleHandler tries to do is to open a network connection to the

Listing 2.

```java
import java.lang.*;
import java.net.*;
import java.util.*;
import java.io.*;

public class simpleClient {
    static int port;
    static String host;

    public static void main(String args[]) {
        try {
            host = args[0];
            port = Integer.parseInt(args[1]);
        } catch (Exception e) {
            host = "localhost";
            port = 13;
        }
        /* Create a new instance of the simpleServer */
        simpleHandler ss = new simpleHandler(host, port);
    }
}

class simpleHandler {
    BufferedInputStream instream;
    Socket conn;

    simpleHandler(String host, int port) {
        try {
            conn = new Socket(host, port);
            instream = new
            BufferedInputStream(conn.getInputStream());
        } catch (Exception e) {
            System.out.println("Err: " + e);
            System.exit(1);
        }
        /* Read line from the socket and then
        write it out */
        String str = this.getline();
        System.out.println("Str: " + str.trim());
    }

    public String getline() {
        StringBuffer strbuf = new StringBuffer();
        int tmp;
        do {
            try {
                /* Try to read from the stream */
                tmp = instream.read();
            } catch(Exception e) {
                return(null);
            }
            if (tmp == -1) {
                /* There is nothing to read */
                return(null);
            }
            if (tmp != 0) {
                /* Add the character */
                strbuf.append((char)tmp);
            }
        } while (tmp != '\n');
        /* Return the String */
        return(strbuf.toString());
    }
}
```

specified host, using the arguments passed from main(). The next line of code tries to establish an input stream from the socket connection in much the same manner that the server examples did in the preceding section. Since both of these calls could generate exceptions, we have used a try...catch statement that will either succeed and the execution of the code will continue, or fail and it will exit reporting the exception to the user by using println().

Once the connection has been established, a call is then made to the getline() method that was first used in a server class and then the line that is returned is printed. In the case of the daytime service this will be the current time and date from the viewpoint of the server.

One of the things that you should note is the amount of replicated code that is shared between the server examples and the client examples. This is a deliberate ploy: we could have written the code to look completely different, but using code that is very similar has the benefit of illustrating the close ties between servers and clients. This is something that should be expected, considering that both types of application are written using the same classes from the same package. This similarity is a great strength of the java.net package, mainly because it uses well-understood principles developed in one area that can be effortlessly deployed in the other.

In fact, the basic principles that apply to servers are exactly the same as those that apply to clients. The essence of the network package is to create a socket (either using a ServerSocket in a server or directly in clients) and then to create the input and output streams using the getInputStream() method and the getOutputStream() method. Once these steps have been taken, it is possible to read and write to the network connections using the methods that we have already illustrated. With this in mind, it is a small matter to create a set of classes and methods that deal with the nitty-gritty of managing network connections, thereby increasing the amount of code that can be reused in a project.

We should also note that the sun.* package hierarchy includes a network library that replicates a good deal of the functionality of the java.net package and often includes classes that are more flexible and require less coding to reach the same level of support. However, since Java ports to other platforms are only required to implement the java.* packages, there is no guarantee that a target system will be able to use the classes in those packages. We have deliberately chosen not to illustrate the use of these

176 DISTRIBUTED COMPUTING

packages for that reason—after all, this article is about the generic Java language and as far as possible is not tied to any specific implementation.

Making Constrained Connections

We have already mentioned the limitations that are imposed on network connections made by applets. However, since it is possible that applet code will be available from a number of servers other than the original distribution point, how is it possible to make connections? One approach is to hard-code the network address of each server into different versions of the applet. Clearly this is a clumsy and inelegant solution. In this section we explain how to obtain the name of the machine that the applet was downloaded from. This can then be used to make a connection that will not fall foul of the security model.

The Applet class contains a number of methods that return information about the document that an applet is embedded in and we will use these to get the information. Listing 3 shows an applet that determines the host from which it was downloaded and then makes a connection to the daytime service, displaying the results using paint().

The most significant lines in the context of this article are

```
URL tt = newURL(this.getDocumentBase(),
      "somefile");
```

and

```
host = tt.getHost();
```

The first line creates a new URL that comprises the document base of the applet (that is, the Web page into which the applet has been embedded) plus a spurious String that is only used to satisfy the parameter requirements of the class. The next line asks the URL for the host element; this is returned as a String. After that, the code is a simple adaptation of the simpleClient class illustrated above ported to be a simple applet.

One potential problem with using this technique to get the hostname is that when pages are loaded from disk (using the "Load File" or similar option) the hostname will be returned as an empty String. This will generate exceptions if passed directly to Socket. Be aware that users may have local copies of your class files, and code accordingly.

THE JAVA.NET LIBRARY 177

Listing 3.

```java
import java.applet.*;
import java.net.*;
import java.io.*;
import java.awt.*;

public class safeConn extends Applet {
    Socket conn;
    int port = 13;
    String host;
    BufferedInputStream instream;
    String time;

    public void init() {
        try {
            URL tt = new
            URL(this.getDocumentBase(),"somefile");
            host = tt.getHost();
        }catch(Exception e) {
            System.out.println("Err: " + e);
        }
        try {
            conn = new Socket(host, port);
            instream = new
            BufferedInputStream(conn.getInputStream());
        } catch (Exception e) {
            System.out.println("Err: " + e);
            System.exit(1);
        }
    }

    public void start() {
        /* Read a line from the socket and
        then write it out */
        time = this.getline();
    }

    public void paint(Graphics g) {
        g.drawString("Host: "+host+" Time: "+time,10,10);
    }

    public String getline() {
        ...
        /* As before in examples */
        ...
    }
}
```

178   DISTRIBUTED COMPUTING

Guidelines for Applets and Applications for Client/Server Applications

The same basic guidelines apply to both servers and clients. For example, it is always preferable to close a socket explicitly using the close() method rather than let it be closed when the application dies or when the connection times out. This is especially important with an applet that must ensure that all open sockets are handled appropriately when the applet is unloaded and reloaded.

Equally, when using network connections, it is essential to keep the user informed of what the applet is doing and why. Recently, there has been increased awareness of the potential for malicious software, and it is prudent both for the prolonged life of your code and for the reputation of yourself and your organization that the user know what connections are being made and why. We would also advise you to avoid hijacking other connections to bypass the security model, for much the same reason. There is no justification for not keeping the user informed of progress and functionality, and a carefully considered approach to this will pay dividends.

GENERAL CONSIDERATIONS

Having discussed some of the specific issues connected with using the java.net package, we now move on to some of the more general issues. These are considerations that are not directly related to the coding of a project, but should be considered when the overall design of the system is being developed.

Network Bandwidth Constraints

One of the biggest problems facing Java and related technologies is the limited capacity of the Internet. Java invites users to download and manipulate a rich content set that can include images, sound clips, and motion video, in addition to the requirement to download the class files associated with the execution of the code.

When designing an applet, you should consider carefully the impact of poor network quality on your application. For example, if your system consists of an applet that feeds back user response to a remote server controlling the animations that are transmitted to the applet, what impact will poor performance have? In this instance, it is easy to imagine that network congestion will delay the user feedback to the server by several seconds. This will frustrate the users as they provide the same feedback again—and when the server gets the messages the action will be executed twice.

Equally, from an attention-span perspective, not many users are going to wait an hour for your meticulously crafted full-motion video to be downloaded over an already crowded network. As a developer, you have but a limited period of time from when the user clicks on the link to your applet to losing interest to show your wares—regardless of whether your content is commercial, educational, or recreational. If you want your applet to be viewed, then carefully consider how you can minimize the amount of network resources you will consume.

One approach that is being considered on a project one of us is involved with is to have the user install the majority of bespoke classes in advance of using the applet. However, this approach is not suitable for every application; this project is supporting many tens of thousands of users and the applet code will frequently be reused. Another approach is to optimize the structure of the code to use as many components as possible from the standard Java packages. While this may force a slightly more generic appearance on applets, it does significantly reduce the network demand.

Whatever way you decide to optimize your applet, it is worth doing. The amount of time it takes for a user to become bored is very short, and to capture the imagination in spite of generally poor network access is a skill that is worth honing.

Good Behavior

Another aspect of using the network library is to ensure that the user has control over the network processes. For example, if you wrote some code that played an audio stream over the network as it was downloaded, you should also take precautions to ensure that the user can control what could be an irritating behavior. If the audio stream accompanied a transcript of a speech, a user visiting the software in a shared office may well want to switch off the audio and concentrate on the text. In our experience, there is no other aspect of control in software that is more overlooked or underestimated than network connections. When writing any kind of code, make sure that the user has control and not the developer. Users who get tired of software will not revisit it.

180 DISTRIBUTED COMPUTING

We are indebted to Addison–Wesley Longman for permission to reproduce an edited version of chapter 8 from *Active Java* by Adam Freeman and Darrel Ince. Copyright © 1996, Addison–Wesley Longman. Limited.

Adam Freeman is a software consultant working in the Knowledge Media Institute at the Open University. He is a member of the team developing Stadium, one of the largest Java applications in the world, and is an Advisor to the Board of SunWorld Online. Darrel Ince is a Professor of Computing at the Open University. He is an accomplished author of more than 100 research papers and 18 books on software subjects.

SECTION EIGHT

PERSISTENCE

Making Java Objects Persistent

Patrick O'Brien

THE LIFETIME OF a persistent object exceeds the life of the application process that created it. Persistent object management is the mechanism for storing the state of objects in a non-volatile place so that when the application shuts down, the objects continue to exist.

As a Java programmer, you may choose several different options when determining how to satisfy your persistent object management needs. We will look at four approaches in this article: Serialization, Persistent Storage Engine, JDBC, and Object Databases.

The simplest approach is to use the file system directly. Fortunately, Java provides Object Serialization which helps handle the flattening of objects into streams. These streams can be written to files and then subsequently read to reconstruct your program's objects.

Although Serialization is easy to use, you may run into performance problems with large numbers of objects. There is a new class of software called a Persistent Storage Engine (PSE) that improves upon some of the limitations of Serialization. With a PSE you do not incur the additional learning curve that a full database management system product requires. Like Serialization, a PSE transparently writes objects to disk, but a PSE also provides reliable storage and better performance for large numbers of objects.

When your application has to support large numbers of concurrent users, you will probably want to consider moving up to a Database Management System (DBMS). With Java there are two different categories of databases to choose from: Relational databases and Object databases. The

184   PERSISTENCE

JDBC interface, developed by JavaSoft, provides a standard way to access Relational databases from Java. For Object databases, ODMG, with assistance from JavaSoft, is producing a standard Java binding that several vendors will be supporting.

The option that is right for you depends on the requirements of your application. For most applications, there are four key criteria for success that drive the decision making process:

1. Achieving performance and scalability goals
2. Satisfying reliability and availability requirements
3. Minimizing development costs and meeting time-to-market constraints
4. Managing the cost of deployment and administration

The four options for Java persistence vary considerably in their ability to satisfy these criteria under different application workloads. So, before choosing a strategy for persistent object management, you have to understand the intended use. For example, when purchasing a new vehicle, the sales person would want to know whether you want to haul gravel or take home the groceries before recommending a station wagon over a dump truck. In the same way, when choosing your approach to persistent object management, you will want to know how many users will be concurrently accessing the data; how much data needs to be stored; how complex is the object model; what are the availability needs; and so on.

In this article we examine the Java programmer's different options, assess the option's strength and weaknesses, and provide criteria to help choose which option will meet your specific application requirements.

OPTIONS FOR JAVA PERSISTENCE

To help illustrate the different options for Java persistence, we will use a common code example throughout this article. The example will focus on storing employee information. The Java code for the Employee class is shown below:

```
public class Employee {
        String name;
        int age;
        int salary;
        Employee manager;
```

```
    // constructor
    public Employee(String name,
                    int age,
                    int salary,
                    Employee manager) {
        this.name = name;
        this.age = age;
        this.salary = salary;
        this.manager = manager;
    }
}
```

OBJECT SERIALIZATION

Typically, Object Serialization is used to store copies of objects in a file, or to ship copies of objects to code running in another Java virtual machine. Serialization enables you to flatten objects into a stream of bytes that, when later read, will recreate objects equivalent to those that were written to the stream. Object Serialization is currently available as a beta release that works with JDK 1.0.2 and is scheduled to be released as part of JDK 1.1.

Serialization defines interfaces for writing and reading objects, and classes that implement those interfaces. When you write an object to an object output stream, a byte stream is generated. The byte stream can be read by a corresponding object input stream to create a new object that is equivalent to the original object.

In the JDK 1.1 release, there is a new class attribute, serializable, that you can use to mark those classes which may be serialized. You do not have to write special code to allow a class to be serialized—you simply set the serializable flag in the class. A default mechanism is provided for the flagged class. The default mechanism implements writeObject and readObject methods that write (read) each field of the object. You can customize the serialization by writing your own per class implementations.

Writing objects to a stream is a straightforward process. To serialize an Employee we do the following:

```
Employee e = new Employee ("John Smith", 99, 75000, null);
FileOutputStream f = new FileOutputStream("tmp");
ObjectOutput s = new ObjectOutputStream(f);
s.writeObject(e);
s.flush();
```

186 PERSISTENCE

First an OutputStream, in this case a FileOutputStream, is needed to receive the bytes. Then an ObjectOutputStream is created that writes to the OutputStream. Next, the Employee e, and objects reachable from e, are written to the stream. Objects are written with writeobject which serializes the specified object, and traverses its references to other objects in the object graph, recursively, to create a complete serialized representation of the graph.

Reading an object from a stream is equally straight forward:

```
// Deserialize an Employee from a file.
FileInputStream in = new FileInputStream("tmp");
ObjectInputStream s = new ObjectInputStream(in);
Employee e = (Employee)s.readObject();
```

First an InputStream, in this case a FileInput Stream, is needed as the source stream. Then an ObjectInputStream is created that reads from the InputStream. Next, the Employee object is read from the stream. Objects are read with the readObject method, which deserializes the specified object and traverses its references to other objects recursively to create the complete graph of objects serialized.

STRENGTHS AND WEAKNESSES OF SERIALIZATION

Serialization provides a simple yet extensible mechanism for storing objects persistently. The Java object type and safety properties are maintained in the serialized form and Serialization only requires per class implementation for special customization. Serialization should be sufficient for applications that operate on small amounts of persistent data and in cases where reliable storage is not an absolute requirement.

In contrast, Serialization is not the optimal choice for applications that have to manage megabytes of persistent objects, are frequently updating those objects, or want to ensure that the changes are reliably saved in persistent storage.

Because Serialization has to read/write entire graphs of objects at a time, it works best for small numbers of objects. When the byte stream is a couple of megabytes in size, you may find that storing objects via Serialization is too slow, especially if your application is doing frequent updates that need to be saved. Another drawback is the lack of undo or abort of changes to objects.

Finally, Serialization does not provide reliable object storage. If your system or application crashes during the writeObject call, the contents of the file will be lost. To protect against application or system failures and to ensure that persistent objects are not destroyed, the persistent file has to be copied before each change is saved.

The two key improvements that a Persistent Storage Engine provides over Serialization are better performance for large numbers of objects and reliable object management.

PERSISTENT STORAGE ENGINES

The limitations of Serialization are improved upon by a Persistent Storage Engine. A PSE provides the simplicity and extensibility of serialization while overcoming the reliability and performance problems when managing tens of megabytes of object data.

In this article we will provide an example of a PSE using Object Design's ObjectStore PSE for Java. PSE for Java is the first persistent storage engine written entirely in Java. PSE has a small footprint (less than 250K) when compared with a DBMS, so it can easily be packaged with applications or applets. PSE runs within the same process as the Java application (see Figure 1).

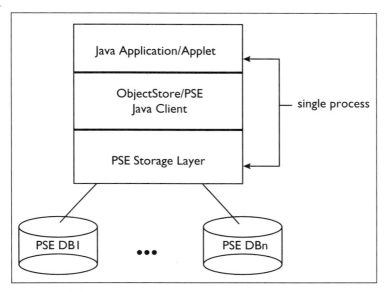

Figure 1. PSE architecture.

188 PERSISTENCE

Similar to Serialization, PSE provides an easy-to-use interface for storing and retrieving Java objects. Persistent Java classes, and their fields and methods, are defined the same way as transient Java classes. The programmer declares classes to be persistent capable and then uses standard Java constructs to create and manipulate both persistent and transient instances. Transparent object persistence through PSE enables developers to make use of the full power of Java and to easily incorporate existing class libraries with PSE.

Database functionality is provided through the PSE for Java API, which primarily provides functions to

- Create, open and close databases
- Start and end transactions
- Store and retrieve persistent objects

PSE automatically generates the equivalent of readObject and writeObject for each persistent-capable class. As with Serialization, developers can override the implementation of these methods.

While Serialization reads and writes complete graphs of objects, PSE provides explicit, fine-grained control over object access and fetching. Single objects can be read from and written to the database. Related objects are automatically fetched when dereferenced by application code.

PSE supports single program access to databases, meaning that a database can be updated by at most one application at one time. Multiple applications can read the same database simultaneously, but only one application can be writing to the database.

A primary difference between Serialization and PSE is evident in the area of transactions and recovery. With Serialization, persistent stores are not automatically recoverable; consequently, in the event of an application or system failure, a file can only be recovered back to the beginning of the application session and only if a copy of the file is made before the application begins.

In contrast, PSE provides automatic database recovery and transactions that support atomic commits. PSE ensures the integrity and reliability of your data, even when your Java application or system fails. In PSE, which does genuine atomic commits, databases are always recoverable at the transaction level. If an application crashes while updating a database, PSE will recover the database up to the last committed transaction. PSE also ensures that either all of your changes are made to the database, or none of your changes are made.

The following programming example illustrates how to create a PSE database with one Employee object that is assigned to a root with name "theBoss."

```
class Example1 {
    public static void main (){

    ObjectStore.initialize(null, null);

    Database db = Database.create ("employee.odb",
        Database.allRead | Database.allWrite);

    Transaction t = Transaction.begin(Transaction.update);
    Employee e = new Employee ("John Smith", 50, 90000, null);

    db.createRoot("theBoss", e);

    t.commit();
    db.close();
    }
}
```

In the above example, the program first initializes the PSE software and then creates and opens a database named "employee.odb." Next, an update transaction is started and a new persistent capable Employee object is created. Then a database root is created with the label "theBoss" and is associated with the Employee object that was previously created. Finally, the transaction is committed and this causes the Employee object to be stored in the database.

STRENGTHS AND WEAKNESSES OF PSE

Like Serialization, PSE is easy to use and fairly transparent for the Java programmer. Objects of any Java class can easily be stored and retrieved in a PSE database.

Unlike Serialization, however, PSE provides explicit, fine-grained control over object access and fetching, resulting in high performance and scalable storage management for large numbers of Java objects. Consequently, ObjectStore PSE will perform well for databases in the "tens of MBs" range. In addition, you should see substantial performance improvements over Serialization even for smaller numbers of objects.

PSE introduces transactions semantics, which is an additional concept for programmers to learn. But the added benefits of transactions and

190 PERSISTENCE

recovery—in particular, data integrity and preventing application and system failures from corrupting databases—are certainly worth the effort for many applications.

When databases start to exceed one hundred MBs, PSE performance will start to degrade. Consequently, you should consider using a full database management system that offers clustering to support finer control over the physical placement of objects.

Also, PSE is not intended for large numbers of concurrent users. It can support multiple readers, but writers will be serialized since locks are held at the database level. If you expect your application to support a high volume of concurrent updates, you will want to consider a full DBMS.

Finally, PSE provides persistent versions of Vector and Dictionary, as well as persistent versions of several collection libraries such as JGL. But these classes are intended for small to medium cardinality collections and do not scale to tens of thousands of instances. If you require high-performance, indexed queries over large collections, you should consider using a full DBMS product instead.

DATABASE MANAGEMENT SYSTEMS

Database Management Systems are intended to support a large number of concurrent users, high volumes of updates, and queries over large collections of objects. A DBMS will ensure the integrity and reliability of your data, and provide full support for administration of the database in a highly available, 7x24, environment.

There are two classes of DBMS that we will consider: Relational databases, which are supported by Java's JDBC API, and Object databases, which are supported through the ODMG's Java binding.

RELATIONAL DATABASES AND JDBC

JavaSoft has introduced a standard SQL database-access interface, the JDBC API. JDBC allows Java programs to issue SQL statements and process the results. This API provides a uniform interface to a wide range of Relational databases, and provides a common base on which higher level tools and interfaces can be built.

JDBC is deliberately a "low level" API that is intended for application builder tools and as a base for higher level APIs. It is based on the XOPEN SQL CLI standard and Microsoft's ODBC standard. Choosing

ODBC was a pragmatic choice since it is a widely accepted and implemented standard for SQL database access. Virtually all databases support ODBC, and it has recently been extended beyond Microsoft platforms to be supported on most Unix platforms as well.

Before looking at the JDBC API, let's first look at how JDBC is being implemented. In Figure 2, the major architectural components of JDBC are shown.

JDBC consists of two main layers: first, the JDBC API, which supports Java application-to-JDBC Driver Manager communications; second, the JDBC Driver API, which supports JDBC Driver Manager-to-ODBC Driver communications. The JDBC Driver Manager is designed to handle communication with multiple drivers of different types. In Figure 2, three different types of drivers are depicted.

The first is the JDBC-ODBC bridge driver which translates JDBC method calls into ODBC function calls. This allows off-the-shelf ODBC drivers to be used, enabling JDBC to leverage the database connectivity provided by the existing array of native ODBC drivers. The JDBC-ODBC bridge is being offered by JavaSoft as part of the JDBC package.

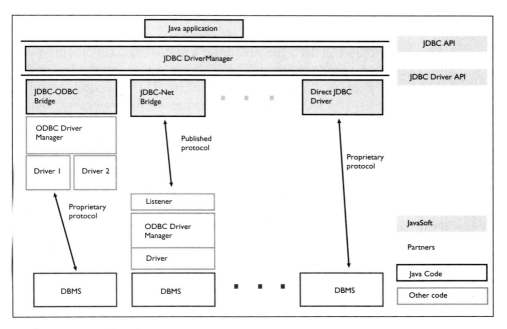

Figure 2. JDBC architecture.

192   PERSISTENCE

The second driver is the JDBC-Net Bridge which, uses a published protocol to communicate with a remote database listener that front ends the ODBC Driver Manager. With this configuration, the client-side is completely written in Java, enhancing portability and removing the need to have drivers for different databases installed on the client.

The last type of bridge is a direct JDBC driver that communicates directly with a specific DBMS, bypassing the ODBC layer. The advantage of supporting this style of bridge is the performance benefit gained from eliminating the ODBC layer.

The JDBC API defines Java classes to represent database connections, SQL statements, result sets, and database metadata. In terms of Java classes, the JDBC API consists of:

- java.sql.Connection
- java.sql.Statement
- java.sql.PreparedStatement
- java.sql.CallableStatement
- java.sql.ResultSet

A Connection represents a session with a specific database. Within the context of a Connection, SQL statements are executed and results are returned.

A Statement object is used for executing a static SQL statement and obtaining the results produced by it. The "executeQuery" method is used for SELECT statements that return a single ResultSet. The "executeUpdate" is used for INSERT, UPDATE, DELETE and other simple statements that do not return results. The "execute" statement is used to handle the more esoteric variations, for example, queries that return multiple results.

An SQL statement can be pre-compiled and stored in a PreparedStatement object. This object can then be used to efficiently execute this statement multiple times. PreparedStatement also adds support for IN parameters. There are a series of setXXX methods (where XXX is one of the JDBC supported data types) that allow you to assign parameters.

CallableStatement extends PreparedStatement for use with stored procedures. It adds support for OUT parameters. You have to first register OUTs using the registerOutParameter method and then retrieve the value after the call execution using one of the getXXX methods.

ResultSet provides access to a table of data generated by executing a SELECT statement. A ResultSet maintains a cursor pointing to its current row of data. Initially the cursor is positioned before the first row. The next method moves the cursor to the next row. The getXXX methods retrieve column values for the current row. You can retrieve values by either using the index number of the column, or by using the name of the column.

The API also contains two classes, java.sql.DatabaseMetaData and java.sql.ResultSetMetaData, that are used for metadata interfaces.

The following example shows a simple query that retrieves all of the Employees in the database.

```
public void doSelect() throws SQLException {
// Open a database connection.
    Connection con =
        DriverManager.getConnection
        ("jdbc:odbc:wombat");

// Create and execute a statement.
    Statement stmt = con.createStatement();
    ResultSet rs = stmt.executeQuery(
        "SELECT emp_name, emp_age, emp_salary FROM employees");

// Step through the result rows.
    while (rs.next()) {
        // get the values from the current row:
        String name = rs.getString("emp_name");
        int age = rs.getInt(2);
        int salary = rs.getInt(3);
        println("name= " + name + ", age= "+ age + ", salary= " + salary);
    }
}
```

STRENGTHS AND WEAKNESSES OF JDBC

Relational databases are mature products with extensive track records in supporting large numbers of concurrent users in high availability production environments. There is an abundance of SQL-based development tools, system administration utilities and end-user access products that support Relational databases.

For many Java applications, access to existing Relational databases will be a requirement and JDBC provides a uniform way to access these databases based on a proven standard. Programmers who are familiar with SQL should be able to quickly learn how to use JDBC.

Java, however, is an object-oriented language. Developers using Java create classes, instantiate objects, and invoke methods. Developers using Relational databases define tables, insert records, and call stored procedures. The impedance mismatch between the object model of Java and the SQL model of a Relational database can adversely affect your ability to satisfy two key criteria: namely, achieving performance goals and minimizing development costs while meeting time-to-market constraints.

Whether you are accessing an existing Relational database, or trying to use a Relational database for persistent storage for your new Java application, mapping Java objects to the flat record model of a Relational database can be problematic.

Depending on the complexity of your application's object model, the mapping code can consume 10–30% of your application code. This results in increased maintenance and debugging costs and can lengthen your time to market.

The cost goes beyond productivity and time to market, however. Flattening objects and mapping them to tables, and then using joins to retrieve records to reconstruct the objects at run time, introduces significant performance overhead. The more complex your application model is, and the more data to you have to access, the greater the performance overhead will be.

Object databases map the object model of your Java program directly into the schema of the Object database. Consequently, there is no mapping code to be written and no flattening/reconstruction overhead at run time. Thus, when contrasted with Relational databases, Object databases can offer significant reductions in development costs and provide substantial improvements in performance for a wide range of Java Internet applications.

OBJECT DATABASES

Since the early 1990s, Object databases have been deployed in a number of mission-critical applications in several vertical markets, such as Telecommunications and Financial Services. Today, most Object databases offer a level of functionality equivalent to Relational databases in terms of supporting large numbers of concurrent users, high availability, reliability, security, query language, development tools and system administration utilities.

The architecture and data model for Object databases are very different from their relational counterparts, however. And it is precisely these differences that provide the performance and time-to-market benefits that many Internet application developers are leveraging today. To illustrate these points, we will use Object Design's ObjectStore DBMS with its new Java interface as an example Object database.

The ObjectStore DBMS delivers high performance object storage coupled with high availability and reliability for both Java and C++ programs. It provides scaleable concurrent access to multiple databases in a distributed multi-tiered environment (see Figure 3). Application developers can take advantage of ObjectStore's complete DBMS capabilities including backup and recovery, security, roll forward, and failover.

The Java interface for ObjectStore API is a superset of the PSE API that we looked at earlier. As with PSE, the schema is generated from Java classes that are marked as persistent capable and there are a small set of classes that provide the interface for the ObjectStore extensions such as databases and transactions. The ObjectStore API is compliant with the ODMG Java binding.

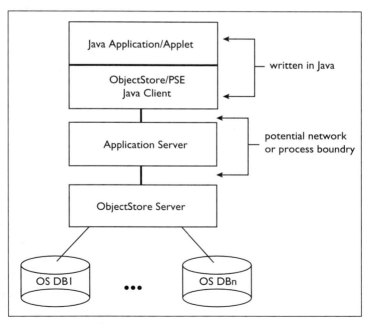

Figure 3. ObjectStore architecture.

196   PERSISTENCE

One of the extensions beyond PSE provided by ObjectStore is a robust collections library that supports storage and indexed associative retrieval of large groups of objects. The library provides arrays, lists, bags, and sets, with b-tree and hash table indexing. ObjectStore provides a query optimizer, which formulates efficient server-side retrieval strategies, minimizing the number of objects examined in response to a query.

Other extensions include a comprehensive library of Object Managers that provide support for multimedia content management. Today's Java applications make extensive use of data types such as image, audio, full text, video and HTML. In addition, specialized data types such as spatial and time series are fully supported. However, support for these extended data types goes beyond storage management. An extended data type will also have sophisticated behavior defined by its methods, such as content-based retrieval of images.

The following is a simple example of an ObjectStore program. It queries an employee database to find the set of employees making less than \$15,000 and prints out the names, salaries, and the managers of those employees.

```
Database db = Database.open ("employee.db", Database.ReadWrite);
Transaction t = Transaction.begin(Transaction.readOnly);

SetOfEmployee employees = (SetOfEmployee)
      db.getRoot("AllEmployees");
SetOfEmployee PoorEmployees =
      employees.query("salary < 15000");
EmployeeEnumeration ei =
      PoorEmployees.elements();

while (ei.hasMoreElements()) {
   Employee e = ei.nextElement();
   System.out.println(e.name + " is a poverty risk with salary " + e.salary);
      System.out.println(e.name + "'s manager is " + e.manager.name); }
t.commit();
db.close();
```

In the above example, the employee.db database is opened and a transaction is started. Then the code retrieves a database root which contains a reference to an ObjectStore collection called AllEmployees. Next the example iterates through all the members of the collection that satisfy the ObjectStore query salary < 15000, and then prints out the name and salary of those employees, and the name of the employee's manager. After the iteration is complete, the transaction is ended and the database is closed.

STRENGTHS AND WEAKNESSES OF OBJECT DATABASES

ObjectStore provides a powerful data management environment for Java applications. It provides a seamless binding to the Java language which results in an easy to use interface that drastically reduces the amount of code required to manage persistent Java objects, while providing developers with the full power of Java to define, manipulate, and share important application data. Creating persistent Java objects using ObjectStore is as easy as creating transient Java objects, which means that the increased productivity of the Java environment is further enhanced with ObjectStore.

As a result of ObjectStore's support for extended data types and the built-in functions that manipulate these types, Java developers can save time by not re-inventing the wheel. In addition, Java developers can easily extend the supplied types or define new types. Extended data types provide great flexibility and freedom by leveraging the extensibility that an object model enables.

Most Internet Java applications are composed of classes that have highly interconnected relationships with other classes: in fact, the object model resembles a web. In addition, these applications support users who browse, search, and navigate for information, presenting new requirements for data access which are not satisfied by the SQL-like query functionality provided by Relational databases.

ObjectStore directly supports the extended relationships inherent in Internet Java applications. It provides high performance browsing, searching, and navigating of these complex object models since relationships between objects are stored directly in the database. By directly supporting extended relationships, the development task is simplified since data is stored in the format that it is used in. Direct support for extended relationships also provides superior performance since there is no need to dynamically build relationships—they are already stored in the database.

Object databases offer measurable savings in development costs while decreasing time-to-market. In addition, many Internet Java applications will realize substantial performance improvements when compared with a Relational database solution.

198   PERSISTENCE

However, Object databases have not yet reached the level of widespread use that Relational databases enjoy. Consequently, finding developers with extensive Object database experience is more difficult than finding developers with SQL expertise. This may add to your start-up development costs and affect time-to-market unless you plan ahead and leverage the Object database vendors' consulting services or the growing number of System Integrators who are well-versed in this technology.

ANALYSIS

To illustrate where each of our different options are applicable, we will use our simple Employee example in a couple of different scenarios.

SCENARIO 1

Suppose the first application you want to develop is a personal Rolodex that will keep track of your business contacts. Assume you want to add some more fields to the Employee class to track the phone number, company name, and job title of the business contacts. Additionally, you want to support a simple indexed lookup for people by name and perhaps company.

You anticipate that the number of contacts at any time will not be greater than a couple of hundred entries. Since this is a personal directory, all access, both read and write, will be from a single user.

For this scenario, Object Serialization would be an adequate solution. The database is small, access is single user, and you are not overly concerned about losing an update or two if the application crashes while you are modifying the Rolodex. Before you update the file, however, you would want to make a copy of it to prevent corrupting the database during an update session. You can build a transient dictionary object when the file is read in to provide indexed lookups.

SCENARIO 2

Now suppose you want to build a company-wide personnel directory, that will store information about employees, their phone numbers, office locations, and the organizations they belong to. The queries are still pretty simple: you want to locate employees by name or office number.

MAKING JAVA OBJECTS PERSISTENT   199

However, in contrast to the personal Rolodex example, now you have thousands to tens of thousands of entries. Access to the directory will be read-only, but lots of users will be accessing the directory concurrently. Changes are handled off-line by a single clerk and updates are made on a copy of the database.

For this scenario, Serialization is not sufficient because it cannot adequately handle medium to large size companies. Reading the complete company file every time would be far too slow. In addition, the update process would need to incrementally commit transactions, every time an employee update is completed. Serialization would be too slow if you write out the complete database after every change or too risky if you waited until all the changes were made. (I'm sure you can recall the pain you've endured after making a couple of hours worth of edits to a document, only to have the machine crash before you saved the file!)

Consequently, Serialization would be rejected for performance and availability/reliability reasons. In contrast, PSE is a great solution for this scenario. PSE can handle the database size and persistent dictionaries can be stored to handle the indexing. In addition, PSE will support large numbers of read-only users, and, with transactions and recovery, the reliability holes associated with Serialization are not a factor.

SCENARIO 3

Now suppose you want to extend the company-wide directory in a couple of ways. First, you want to allow all employees to update their own information. And, second, you want to provide more sophisticated queries, for example, you want to find all of the employees who make more money than their managers.

For this scenario, PSE would not be an adequate option. The first reason is that PSE does not allow concurrent updates, so everyone trying to update the directory would be serialized. Second, PSE does not provide a query facility, so all of the queries would have to programmed by hand.

Thus, PSE would be rejected due to inadequate multi-user scalability and the lack of query support, which affects the cost of development/time-to-market. In contrast, both JDBC and an Object database would work quite well for this scenario. Concurrent updates are handled and the query facilities would allow extensive searching of the database.

200 PERSISTENCE

SCENARIO 4

Now suppose you want to build a Web-based company-wide personnel, facilities, and product-information directory. You need to incorporate rich content and make the application interactive and dynamic. Some of the functionality being considered includes storing employee's pictures with their employee records. Organization charts might be generated on the fly and displayed by a Web browser. Building plans and floor plans are available so that maps can be generated to enable you to find a particular office or conference room. Operations personnel would like to get the latest information on computer equipment, phone lines, network configurations, IP addresses and so on. Employees would like to get detailed information about the company's products, including multimedia promotional material in the form of video, audio, and images.

Although this application sounds ambitious, it is a typical scenario for Java Internet applications that are being built today. It incorporates rich content with an interactive interface and dynamic presentation of information.

Java with JDBC is not the best option for this scenario. This is not because JDBC is a poor SQL interface; rather, the problem is that Relational databases do not satisfy the requirements of this application. This is because Relational databases are not proficient at managing extended data types such as images, text documents, and spatial data. Furthermore, Relational databases are too slow when processing the extended relationships inherent in object data models.

Relational databases do not provide native support for extended data types. They are designed to manage text and numbers—not the rich data types of the Web. Because they support only character strings and numbers, extended data types such as image, audio, full text, and video are not understood by Relational databases. Consequently, sophisticated browsing and searching on the content of images, for example, is not supported.

Several Relational database vendors have announced their intention to support a limited set of new data types, but storing and retrieving extended data types is only part of the solution. Multimedia content has behavior that is peculiar to each individual data type. For example, image data can be compressed, converted, and rendered. Moreover, searching for all images that have sunsets and mountains is a different process from finding all documents that discuss global warming. Relational databases were not designed to support the behavior or functions that are essential to these extended data types.

Another architectural limitation of Relational databases is that only the database vendor can implement or extend a new data type. Adding a new data type or extending an existing data type requires complex C programming at the database kernel level. However, with new Web data types and technologies emerging at an ever-increasing rate, you cannot wait for the database vendor to provide support in a future release for a new data type: You have to be able to add your own; or, better yet, the company that invents the new data type should be able to easily integrate their technology with the database system.

Object databases are extensible systems. Consequently, it is easy to accommodate new data types and technologies while still providing native data type performance. Using ObjectStore, for example, Java developers create their own new data types and functions. Creating new class libraries is a typical part of the object application development process.

In addition to incorporating rich content, the database must handle dynamic aggregation of customized content, which requires rapid database navigation of complex data models. Relational databases fall short with their lack of support for extended relationships. Relational databases are proficient at running queries over large data sets, when the query can be expressed as a SQL statement. For example, a Relational database can promptly return the set of all employees who have been with the company less than 10 years and who make more than $100,000.

However, a complex data model with highly interconnected data can be a performance nightmare for a Relational database. In scenario 4, for example, generating an organizational chart for a large department would be quite time consuming. This requirement is similar to generating a "bill of materials" where there are many nested subparts. Since parent-child relationships are not directly supported, hundreds of index lookups with expensive joins are required to find all of the related subparts.

In contrast, Object databases provide inherent support for extended relationships. They have enjoyed great success in database application segments where traversing complex extended relationships are the key predictor of ultimate performance. Application segments such as network management, derivatives trading, risk analysis, engineering design, and process control all have one thing in common: they require high performance navigation of complex data models. And they all make use of the Object database's inherent support for extended relationships to

202 PERSISTENCE

achieve the scalability they require to deliver high performance solutions to their users.

For most Internet Java applications that require a database management system, the clear choice is an Object database as opposed to a Relational database with JDBC. With an Object database, developers will be better able to satisfy their performance goals, lower their development costs, and meet their time-to-market objectives.

Patrick O'Brien is responsible for Product Management of Object Design's Internet and Java products. He has been involved in Object Technology since 1983, working with Object-Oriented programming languages, programming environments, and databases. He can be reached at obrien@odi.com.

URLs
For more information on Object Serialization
http://chatsubo.javasoft.com/current/serial/index.html
Object Design's ObjectStore PSE for Java
http://www.odi.com/products/
For more information on JGL
http://www.objectspace.com/jgl/
For more information on JDBC
http://splash.javasoft.com/jdbc/
Object Design's ObjectStore DBMS
http://www.odi.com/products/
For more information on ODBMS Standard
http://www.odmg.org/

StoreTable:
A Java Class for Simple
Object Persistence

Robert "Rock" Howard

SERIALIZATION IS A powerful new mechanism in the JDK 1.1 that can be used, among other things, as a simple persistence mechanism for Java objects. Unfortunately, serialization, when used for persistence, is an all or nothing proposition that often does not scale up well. This is especially true for applications in which complex data is updated by relatively small increments. This article introduces StoreTable, a Java class that builds upon the serialization mechanism to provide Java persistence in a more useful and scalable manner.

MORE ABOUT SERIALIZATION

A serialized object is simply a data stream that contains the minimum information that is necessary to reconstruct the object. Note that this information includes not only the values of the direct attributes of the object, but also includes the attributes of the objects that it references and so forth, recursively. The serialization data stream thus includes all the objects that are directly or indirectly linked to the original object.

The new Object Serialization support in the JDK 1.1 is found in the "java.io" package. The ObjectOutputStream class' "writeObject" method and the ObjectInputStream class' "readObject" method are the only methods that were required by StoreTable. There are plenty of other useful aspects of Object Serialization that are not discussed in this article,

204 PERSISTENCE

including security options, versioning, and the ability to customize the serialization process via the Serializable and Externalizable public interfaces. As the JDK documentation explains, the Java support for Object Serialization is sufficient for lightweight persistence of Java objects.

The reason that using serialization for persistence is only appropriate for lightweight persistence is that it generally requires that an object be saved or recalled in its entirety. This is counterproductive for small updates to objects with many complex links to other objects. Using serialization in such a case would be like requiring a text editor to read every file on a disk into memory before allowing any changes to be made to a single file—and then saving all the files again, even for minor updates. This is rarely a useful approach to data storage.

OTHER CHOICES FOR JAVA PERSISTENCY

If serialization is not effective for saving Java objects, then what other choices are available? Patrick O'Brien tackled this topic in his article entitled "Making Java Objects Persistent" in the January '97 issue of *Java Report*. He reported that a variety of mechanisms including JDBC, ODBs, and PSEs (persistent storage engines) are available for persistence. All of these mechanisms are useful. Your choice depends on your particular requirements for speed and scalability.

Of the alternatives to serialization, the PSE is the most lightweight and offers the best solution on a cost basis for most applications. A good PSE includes several database-like capabilities including transaction management, enhanced security and so forth. What may be less clear is that it is easy to implement a simple and cheap PSE without these more advanced capabilities by building upon the serialization capability to implement a persistent data structure such as a persistent hash table. That is the approach that we take in the StoreTable class.

A BARE BONES PERSISTENT STORAGE ENGINE

First consider the use of a hash table within an object-oriented application. Objects that are to be saved in the table are keyed to a name in some well-defined manner. Given the name, the hash table determines a slot within the table where the object will be saved. Generally this is done by saving a reference to the object in the assigned slot. The key name is used later to retrieve the object reference from the table. Note that if we simply serialize this hash table, then not only the hash table, but all of the objects held within the table would be serialized in one fell swoop.

In StoreTable we also save objects into a hash table, but instead of storing an object reference, we serialize the object into a file and save the name of the file in the hash table. Now if we serialize the hash table, then the saved serialized hash table will include only the filenames of the saved objects and not the objects themselves. If we restore a StoreTable from disk, then we are restoring only the table of filenames. The individual objects are not restored to memory until they are fetched from the StoreTable by name.

THE STORETABLE INTERFACE

The key aspects of the StoreTable interface are shown in Listing 1. The methods shown in the listing allow you to query for items and keys and perform operations that add, delete, or update table entries. We will take a brief look at each of these features.

First, however, I would like to point out that the original implementation of StoreTable was written in the Eiffel programming language. Eiffel directly supports the notion of inheritable assertions in the form of preconditions and postconditions. These are boolean expressions that should be true upon entry and exit of a method call. Most object methodologies now support the definition of preconditions and postconditions and, in our experience, they are highly recommended as a mechanism for verifying and documenting method calls.

I point this out because I will be mentioning the assertions that are associated with some of the methods. Keep in mind that if a precondition fails, it's the fault of the caller of the method. If a postcondition fails, it is due to a fault in the method itself. This simple fact, combined with the willingness to define assertions in the first place, can regularly save you from lengthy debugging sessions. As you will see, the preconditions and postconditions are not explicitly defined in the Java implementation of StoreTable due to the execution overhead that this would entail.

THE CONSTRUCTOR

The constructor takes a string as its single argument. This string is the prefix that will be prepended to each file saved by the StoreTable. The

206 PERSISTENCE

Listing 1.

```
public class StoreTable {

    protected int count;

    public StoreTable( String the_filename_prefix )

    /** Set the path in which the files are stored. */
    public void set_path( String new_path )

    /** Returns the object identified by 'an_item' */
    protected Object item( Object key )

    /** Returns a list of all the keys */
    public Enumeration keys()

    /** Is the key in the table?? */
    public boolean has( Object key )

    /** Insert the object in the list */
    public void insert( Object key, Object object )

    /** Replace the object in the list by the new object */
    public void replace( Object key, Object object )

    /** Remove the object from the list */
    public void remove( Object key )

} // class StoreTable
```

precondition is that the string exists and is three characters long. (This precondition could be loosened on some operating systems.)

THE QUERY OPERATIONS

The "has" method checks whether the supplied key is already in the table. The precondition is that the key exists.

The "item" method returns the object associated with a supplied key. The precondition is that the key exists and that the StoreTable has an item associated with the given key. The postcondition is that the returned item is not void.

The "keys" method returns an Enumeration that yields the current set of keys in use in the table.

The "count" field specifies how many keys are currently in use in the table.

StoreTable: A Java Class for Simple Object Persistence   207

Listing 2.

```java
import java.util.*;
import java.lang.String;
import java.io.*;

public class StoreTable {

    protected Hashtable table;
    protected String filename_prefix;
    protected String path;
    protected int count;
    protected int file_counter;

    public StoreTable( String the_filename_prefix )
    {
        count = 0;
        table = new Hashtable( 113, 5 );
        filename_prefix = new String( the_filename_prefix );
        path = new String( "" );
    }

    /** Set the path in which the files are stored.
    */
    public void set_path( String new_path )
    {
        path = new String( new_path );
    }

    /** Should only be done once...
    */
    protected String lockfilename()
    {
        String Result;

        Result = new String( path ).concat( filename_prefix )
                .concat( "index" );

        return Result;
    }

    /** Keep trying until you can lock
    */
    protected void lock()
    {
        while( lock_attempt() ){
            // do_nothing();
        }
    }
    /** If lockfile doesn't exist, create it and return False
    */
    protected boolean lock_attempt()
    {
        File lockfile;
        FileOutputStream lock;
        boolean Result;

        lockfile = new File( lockfilename() );
        Result = lockfile.exists();

        if( !Result ){
            try{
                lock = new FileOutputStream( lockfile );
                lock.close();
            }
            catch( IOException e ){
                System.out.println("IO Error occurred !!" );
                Result = true;
            }
        }
        return Result;
    }
    protected void  release_lock()
    {
        File lockfile;
        lockfile = new File( lockfilename() );
        lockfile.delete();
    }

    /** Returns the object identified by 'an_item'
    */
    protected Object item( Object key )
    {
        Object Result;
        String filename = (String) table.get( key );

        lock();
        try{
            FileInputStream istream = new FileInputStream
                                    ( path+filename );
            ObjectInputStream storer = new ObjectInputStream
                                    ( istream );

            Result = storer.readObject();
        }
        catch( Exception e ){
            Result = null;
            System.out.println( e.toString() );
        }
        release_lock();

        return Result;
    }

    /** Returns a list of all the keys
    */
    public Enumeration keys()
    {
        return table.keys();
    }

    /** Is the key in the table??
    */
    public boolean has( Object key )
    {
        boolean Result;

        lock();
        Result = table.contains( key );
        release_lock();

        return Result;
    }

    /** Insert the object in the list
    */
    public void insert( Object key, Object object )
    {
        String filename = determine_filename( key );

        lock();

        try{
            FileOutputStream ostream = new FileOutputStream
                                    ( path+filename );
            ObjectOutputStream storer = new ObjectOutputStream
                                    ( ostream );

            table.put( key, filename );
            storer.writeObject( object );
        }
        catch( IOException e ){
            System.out.println( e.toString() );
        }
        release_lock();
        count = count + 1;
    }

    /** Replace the object in the list by the new object
```

208 PERSISTENCE

Listing 2. continued.

```java
*/
public void replace( Object key, Object object)
{
    String filename = (String) table.get( key );

    lock();

    try{
        FileOutputStream ostream = new FileOutputStream
                                   ( path+filename );
        ObjectOutputStream storer = new ObjectOutputStream
                                    ( ostream );

        storer.writeObject( object );
    }
    catch( IOException e ){
        System.out.println( e.toString() );
    }
    release_lock();
}

/** Remove the object from the list
*/
public void remove( Object key )
{
    File file;

    lock();
    file = new File( path + (String)table.get( key ));
    file.delete();
    table.remove( key );
    count = count - 1;
    release_lock();
}

/** Determines the filename of the 'key'
*/
protected String determine_filename( Object key )
{
    String Result;

    Result = new String( filename_prefix ).concat( translate
                                  ( file_counter ));
    file_counter = file_counter + 1;

    return Result;
}

protected String translate( int n )
{
    int rest = n;
    int mychar = 0;
    String Result = new String( "" );
    String tmp;

    for( rest = n; rest >= 26; ){
```

```java
        mychar = (rest / 26) + 1;
        rest = rest % 26;

        if( Result.length() ==0 ){
            Result = Result.concat( new String().valueOf( (char)
                                        (mychar + 96)) );
        }
        else{
            tmp = new String().valueOf( (char)(mychar + 96) ).
                                        concat(Result);

            Result = tmp;
        }
    } // for-loop

    if( Result.length() ==0 ){
        Result = Result.concat( new String().valueOf( (char)
                                        (rest + 97)) );
    }
    else{
        tmp = new String().valueOf( (char)(rest + 97) ).concat
                                        (Result);

        Result = tmp;
    }

    while( Result.length() < 5 ){
        tmp = new String("a").concat(Result);
        Result = tmp;
    }

    return Result;
}

} // class StoreTable

public class Stest {
//  protected StoreTable STable;

    public Stest(){}
    public static void main(String argv[])
    {
        StoreTable STable = new StoreTable( "Gwm" );

        String item = new String("ID");
        String item2 = new String( "Junk" );

        STable.insert( item, new String("Done") );
        STable.insert( new String("BC"), new String("DE") );
        STable.insert( new String("ABCDE"), new String("DEFGH") );

        item2 = (String) STable.item( item );
        System.out.println( item2 );

        STable.remove( item );
    }
}
```

THE UPDATE OPERATIONS

The "insert" operation takes a key and an object and persistently saves the object such that the object is associated with the supplied key. The preconditions are that the key exists, the object exists, and that the supplied key is not already in use in the table. The postconditions are that the table now contains the supplied key and that the supplied key is bound to the supplied object.

The "replace" operation is identical to "insert" except for the precondition that key already is in use within the table.

The "remove" operation disassociates the key from the table and also deletes the associated persistent object. The precondition is that the key exists and that it is currently in use within the table.

THE DESIGN OF STORETABLE

We designed the class interface such that the update operations change the state of the StoreTable, but do not return any state information. By contrast, the query operations return state information but do not change the state of the StoreTable. Many OO experts recommend segregating class interfaces in this manner and, in our own experience, this is the best way to create minimal, but complete, class interfaces. As the number of methods in a class grows, this design principle often ends up being violated, but we still find this simple rule to be a useful guide when designing Java classes.

The StoreTable interface hides a lot of complexity. This includes:

1. The mapping of the object keys to the saved files. In particular, the filenames are generated automatically.
2. The saving and restoration of the table index.
3. The file locking mechanism and logic.

The interface could actually be simplified further (and perhaps made more robust) by having the constructor require both the filename prefix string and the path to be supplied. With this change, the "set_path" method could be eliminated.

Besides the aspects mentioned previously, there are several other assumptions coded into the StoreTable including:

210   PERSISTENCE

1. The table is locked whenever the table index is accessed and for the entire duration of the following methods: "keys," "has," "insert," "replace," and "remove."
2. We assume that the default size and operation of the HashTable is appropriate for a program using StoreTable.
3. We assume that the program has the necessary permissions that are required in order to create files in the directory where the table objects are saved, as well as permission to read, replace, and delete these files.

A minor drawback in the supplied code in Listing 2 is that the mechanism for handling failed lock attempts is not fully realized. If an attempt to grab a lock fails, then the code falls into a forever loop that continually attempts to grab the lock. This is one of many areas that would need attention in order to upgrade the StoreTable into an industrial PSE. Other desired capabilities include a transaction management layer for committing updates and performing rollbacks as well as a security layer for fine-tuning data access and update security beyond the primitive level supplied by the underlying file system.

The StoreTable class can serve as a template for creating other types of storage engines by replacing the persistent hash table with some other data structure such as a balanced tree or a directed graph. In fact, the beauty of combining small but powerful components in the manner of StoreTable is not so much the cost savings (you can't beat "free"), but in the ability to quickly respond to changing requirements.

Of course it is the availability of robust high-level classes for data structures, serialization and file management that make the StoreTable possible. This is yet another brilliant demonstration of the strength of object-oriented programming—particularly when plenty of powerful libraries are available to draw upon. It is encouraging to discover new solutions that are built through minor extension of existing technology, especially when you know that these solutions can be easily and flexibly adapted to new uses in the future.

FOR THE RECORD

StoreTable was first invented in Eiffel by Marco Keja at the suggestion of yours truly and with additional design input from Bart Roelofsma. The coding in Eiffel took one week and additional testing, documentation, and further refinement took another week. See the Eiffel column in the June 1997 issue of *JOOP* for more details about the Eiffel version of StoreTable.

The translation to Java was performed by Gerwin Mulder. This effort took one day and resulted in the StoreTable.java class that is presented in Listing 2. It turns out that Eiffel and Java are surprisingly similar in many respects. We have found that much of our Eiffel technology has been easy to transport to Java.

The Eiffel and Java versions of StoreTable are available for free download from the Tower Technology Web site. We hope that you find the StoreTable code useful. Please send any comments or suggestions about the code to me at rock@twr.com.

Robert "Rock" Howard is the Chief Technology Officer at Tower Technology Corporation in Austin, TX. Mr. Howard can be reached via email at rock@twr.com. Tower's Web site is http://www.twr.com.

SECTION NINE

LESSONS LEARNED

Upgrading Your Web Site to Java: The First Step

Lowell Kaplan

There is a lot of hype about what Java can do to improve a Web site; however, most sites still use HTML and CGI. This article presents the combination of a Java client with CGI on the server side as the first step on the path to upgrading a Web site. The future of Java on the server side is also reviewed.

THERE ARE a great many Web sites on the Internet that do an outstanding job of presenting static information, typically either text or pictures. There are even some sites that allow you enter data about yourself, or request information of some kind, or even search the Web for a particular topic. These Web sites use HTML, and the more advanced ones, which allow the submission of data, use Common Gateway Interface (CGI) programming on the back end. They are certainly adequate for simple distribution of information, but do not offer much in the way of dynamic content or interactivity. The introduction of the Java programming language has enabled developers to write full-fledged applications, which can be run over the Internet. The question now arises: How does one go about migrating a Web site from mostly static HTML and CGI to interactive Java?

First, a Web site can be broken down into two major components: the client (front end) and the server (back end). The client is the user interface that is seen by users in their Web browsers, and the server is the program running on the Web server machine. The server is typically responsible for file loading and saving, database searches, and other data processing tasks. The server performs these tasks, and then sends the results to the client so the user can see the results. Traditional Web sites have used

216 LESSONS LEARNED

HTML to program the client and a CGI program for the server. So, the first step in upgrading a Web site to Java is to determine how Java can fulfill the requirements on both the client side and the server side.

One of the major issues Java developers have had to deal with is Java's security restriction prohibiting local file access from applets. Many applications have a need to save and load data to and from files. A commonly implemented solution to this problem is to write two programs, a Java client that runs as an applet in a browser, and a Java server that is a stand-alone Java application running on the Web server machine. Because the server program is an application, it is able to read and write files. So, when a client program wants to access a file, it must open a connection to the server program, and then send or receive the data. The problem with this approach is that this server must always be up and running on the Web server machine, always waiting for a client to open a connection to it. Not only does this add the additional overhead of an extra program running on the Web server machine, but consider what happens when there is another program that also needs a server to read and write files. Eventually, one could end up with dozens of little server programs, each listening on a port of the Web server machine, each one adding to the server's workload.

THE NEXT STEP

So, what's the alternative? The answer is surprising. Basically, what is needed is a program that is always running on the Web server machine and has the ability to access local files. There is already a program that does this: the Web server itself. In fact, there is even a standard way to run a program on the server machine going through the Web server; it's called CGI. It may seem strange for a Java solution to use CGI. After all, CGI was the way static HTML Web pages used to get the little bit of dynamic behavior and interactivity they had before Java came along. Now, though, the two technologies can effectively be used in tandem.

The use of CGI programs has some tradeoffs of which one should be aware. The programs are typically written in Perl or C. C as a language is faster than Java because it is a compiled language. Both Perl and Java are interpreted languages, which are slower than compiled languages. Perl, though, was written with text manipulation in mind, so it is optimized for simple tasks such as file saving and loading. Therefore, Perl is also often faster than Java. However, because CGI programs are not written in Java, they lose the portability that Java offers. The same code that runs a Java program under Windows will also run under UNIX. A C program, for example, would have to be recompiled, and possibly edited, for it to be moved from Windows to UNIX. This is not too much of a drawback for CGI, though, because this will only be an issue if the Web server is relocated to another operating system. The client is written in Java, because this is the piece that may need to run in a heterogeneous operating system environment such as the World Wide Web. Another drawback of CGI is that it is limited to HTTP transmissions. These are typically client push, server response interactions. However, for simple tasks like file access, this is all that is necessary.

So, how does a Java applet call a CGI program? The sample code in Listing 1 demonstrates how to call a CGI program, send it parameters, and receive the results. The program itself is just a guestbook program written in Java; it allows users to enter their names, addresses, etc. This does not necessarily harness the full power of a Java client because the same functionality can be achieved using just HTML, but it does demonstrate the techniques that are used.

The saveData() method does the work of calling the CGI program. It first opens a URLConnection to the CGI program's URL. It then gets an OutputStream from this connection that allows it to send data to the CGI program. The data is sent using the POST method as opposed to the GET method, so there is no restriction on how much data can be sent. The data is sent in name-value pairs, the same way HTML forms send data. The syntax is "name=value&name=value& ... &name=value." The values, as you can see in the code, are not directly sent. The static method URLEncoder.encode is called on the values. This method encodes the characters in the value so they can be transmitted through HTTP. This is due to the fact that certain characters in the value could cause problems, like spaces, or extra = or & characters.

In order to make the Java version more valuable than an ordinary HTML page, this program could be enhanced to add a simple validation routine. The validateData() method would be called prior to calling the saveData() method, and it could check to make sure that none of the fields are blank, or that the e-mail address is in the form name@domain, or whatever other validation might be possible on the client side. Previously, all validation had to be done by the CGI program on the server, because this type of advanced programming logic could not be accomplished with HTML. In the CGI scenario, all the data needed to be sent to the server,

218 LESSONS LEARNED

Listing 1.

```java
import java.awt.*;
import java.applet.*;
import java.io.*;
import java.net.*;

public class GuestBook extends Applet
{
    TextField nameField;
    TextField address1Field;
    TextField address2Field;
    TextField cityField;
    TextField stateField;
    TextField zipField;
    TextField phoneField;
    TextField emailField;

    Button saveButton;

    public void init()
    {
        createControls();
    }

    private void createControls()
    {
        setLayout(new BorderLayout());

        Panel dataPanel = new Panel();
        dataPanel.setLayout(new GridLayout(8,2));
        dataPanel.add(new Label("Name"));
        dataPanel.add(nameField = new TextField(20));
        dataPanel.add(new Label("Address 1"));
        dataPanel.add(address1Field = new TextField(20));
        dataPanel.add(new Label("Address 2"));
        dataPanel.add(address2Field = new TextField(20));
        dataPanel.add(new Label("City"));
        dataPanel.add(cityField = new TextField(20));
        dataPanel.add(new Label("State"));
        dataPanel.add(stateField = new TextField(20));
        dataPanel.add(new Label("Zip Code"));
        dataPanel.add(zipField = new TextField(20));
        dataPanel.add(new Label("Phone"));
        dataPanel.add(phoneField = new TextField(20));
        dataPanel.add(new Label("Email"));
        dataPanel.add(emailField = new TextField(20));

        Panel buttonPanel = new Panel();
        saveButton = new Button("Save");
        buttonPanel.add(saveButton);

        add("Center", dataPanel);
        add("South", buttonPanel);
    }

    public boolean action(Event evt, Object arg)
    {
        if (evt.target == saveButton)
        {
            saveData();
            return true;
        }
    }
```

```java
        return super.action(evt,arg);
    }

    private void saveData()
    {
        try
        {
            //create URL connection to CGI program
            //this is just a sample URL string, it doesn't actually exist
            URL url = new URL("http://www.randomwalk.com/
                                  cgi-bin/savedata.cgi");
            URLConnection connection = url.openConnection();
            connection.setDoOutput(true);

            //create output stream through which to send
            //parameters (POST)
            PrintStream outStream = new PrintStream
                            (connection.getOutputStream());

            //send the data
            outStream.print("name=" + URLEncoder.encode(name-
                Field.getText()) + "&");
            outStream.print("address1=" + URLEncoder.encode
                (address1Field.getText()) + "&");
            outStream.print("address2=" + URLEncoder.encode
                (address2Field.getText()) + "&");
            outStream.print("city=" + URLEncoder.encode
                (cityField.getText()) + "&");
            outStream.print("state=" + URLEncoder.encode(state-
                Field.getText()) + "&");
            outStream.print("zip=" + URLEncoder.encode
                (zipField.getText()) + "&");
            outStream.print("phone=" + URLEncoder.encode
                (phoneField.getText()) + "&");
            outStream.print("email=" + URLEncoder.encode
                (emailField.getText()));

            outStream.close();

            //create input stream to read data back from CGI program
            DataInputStream inStream = new DataInputStream
                (connection.getInputStream());
            String inputLine;

            while ((inputLine = inStream.readLine()) != null)
            {
                //do something with the data which is returned
                System.out.println(inputLine); //print the data
            }
            inStream.close();
        }
        catch (MalformedURLException e)
        {
            e.printStackTrace(System.err);
        }
        catch (IOException e)
        {
            e.printStackTrace(System.err);
        }
    }
}
```

the program had to determine that there was an error, and the new error page had to be sent back to the client. The user, meanwhile, had to wait for all of this to happen, find out that the submission was rejected, and submit the data again after the problem was fixed. Client side validation can provide the user with immediate feedback that a problem exists and how to fix it, without wasting time sending data back and forth to the server. So in general, one should try to do as much client side validation as possible.

There is also a drawback to using CGI scripts written in C or Perl that holds true whether the front end is written in HTML or Java. This has to do with maintenance of the code and keeping all the different pieces synchronized. For example, the client sends data to the CGI program in name-value pairs. If one wants to change one of the variable names, then not only must the client code be changed, but also the CGI program must be changed to recognize the new name. An analogous situation would exist if one wanted to add another piece of data to the screen: both the client and the server code need to be changed and kept in sync. But what can be done to fix this? Well, in an ideal world both the client and the server would be written in an object-oriented language. This way one could write an Entry class, for example, that knows how to both send itself out to a stream, and also knows how to create a new instance of itself reading from a stream. This class would be used by the programs on both the client and the server. Then, changes like those described above could just be made to this one class, and the client and the server would always remain synchronized.

THE FUTURE

As mentioned earlier, running Java programs on the front end and the back end is possible by running a Java program as a standalone application on the server machine. This solution is not ideal for reasons already discussed. However, thanks to some new technological innovations, it is possible to gain the benefits of server side Java programming without the drawbacks. There is the idea of servlets, wherein the Web server has a Java virtual machine built into it. Special HTML pages can be written in which calls to Java programs, or servlets, are embedded with special tags. When the Web server is asked for this type of page, it knows that it needs to run the Java programs specified within the special tags. It takes the output of the Java program and inserts it into the HTML page. Sun

220   LESSONS LEARNED

Microsystems has written a Web server, the "Java Web Server," which supports the use of servlets.

Another new technology from Art Technology Group (ATG), called Dynamo, works in a similar fashion to the Java Web Server. A separate server (the Dynamo server) is run alongside the Web server. The Web server knows that when it is asked to serve up certain file types, it should just pass them along to the Dynamo server. Dynamo then parses the file, checking for a special tag which indicates that the code within the tag is actual Java source code. This code is run through the virtual machine in Dynamo, and the output of the Java code is inserted into an HTML file, which is then returned to the Web server. These two approaches are very similar, and they both allow the use of Java programming on the server side.

Table 1 shows the advantages and disadvantages of these three stages for your Web site. The HTML and CGI combination is the best in terms of wide usability on the client side. It is the only one that is guaranteed to run on all client browsers and operating systems, 16-bit or 32-bit. However, it does not have any of the rest of the features that a Java front end has, like an interactive client program and client side validation. In addition, neither solution with a CGI back end offers the advantages that Java on the front and back end does, including a cross-platform server program, server side data pushes, and object level transports. Asynchronous server side data push is useful in a multi-user environment, where the server needs to notify multiple clients of an event. An example of this is a chat program, where one client sends some text to the server, and the server then sends that text to all of the other clients in the same chat room. So, as the chart indicates, a Java front end/CGI back end is an improvement over a simple HTML/CGI Web site, but still does not have the kind of capabilities that Java on both the client and the server has. The main benefit of using this as an intermediate solution is that it is directly on the path of the desired eventual solution.

THE MIGRATION PATH

Migrating a Web site from purely HTML and CGI to Java on the front and back end can now be achieved incrementally. The first step is to update the client side. Writing a Java front end that still communicates through CGI to an existing back end is a manageable task. One fear of upgrading to a Java client is that there is still a reasonably large segment

Table 1. Availability of Web site features, by technology.

Feature	HTML/CGI	Java/CGI	Java/Java
Client program works on any 32-bit platform (i.e., Windows 95, Windows NT, UNIX, Macintosh, etc.)	yes	yes*	yes*
Interactive client program	no	yes	yes
Client side validation possible	no	yes	yes
Server program works on any 32-bit platform	no	no	yes
Asynchronous server side data pushes	no	no	yes
Supports object level transports (i.e., CORBA, RMI, Object Serialization)	no	no	yes

* Also requires a Java capable browser

of Internet users not using a Java-enabled browser or operating system. Fortunately, there is a way to have Java-enabled users see the Java client, and for the rest of the users to get the HTML version automatically. If Java is not supported in the page that contains the call to the Java applet, it will execute the HTML code up until the closing </APPLET> tag. So, all of the existing HTML code can still be present for those users without Java capabilities, but the <APPLET> tag can be wrapped around it so that the Java version will be run when possible. Another option is to provide the HTML version by default, and offer a clickable link to a Java version of the page. This puts the control in the users' hands. Either way, both the Java version and the HTML version of the client can talk to the same CGI programs on the back end.

Once a Java front end is established, the back end can be addressed. Upgrading the back end to Java may not be feasible immediately, because these server side Java solutions are still very new and may change in the near future. But eventually, writing Java servlets to accomplish back end processing will provide a more robust, cross-platform solution.

Lowell Kaplan is a consultant for Random Walk Computing, Inc., a New York-based firm specializing in Java applications development. He can be reached at lkaplan@randomwalk.com

Java Training Without Getting Soaked

David Moskowitz

BEFORE JAVA, I recommended that our clients who really wanted to learn object-oriented programming should start with Smalltalk as a pure object-oriented environment. If, after Smalltalk, they wanted to move to C++ (though few did), fine. I thought Smalltalk was a much better learning environment to discover objects than C++.

Java shares much of the benefits of Smalltalk when it comes to learning object-oriented programming. It is much harder to write "C with classes" in Java (compared to C++). Java is well suited to learning OO with a benefit that folks that already know C++ (and to a lesser extent C) will feel somewhat comfortable with Java's syntax .

It is not difficult to learn Java. However, it does take time! It also takes an understanding that "Once is not enough." Learning Java is somewhat like mountain weather with time measured in Web years—wait a Web year and there will be something new. The language is not static! To help make a point: Sun recently released version 1.1 and is already talking about improvements in security, lightweight components (e.g., new UI changes including tabbed folders), Java Foundation Classes, and more, starting this summer (3Q97).

What can the beginner do to learn Java? What can an experienced Java programmer do to stay current? How can we do this and not spend ridiculous sums on training? This article focuses on these and related questions.

224 LESSONS LEARNED

GETTING THE MESSAGE

The first question you should ask is: What is the purpose of Java training? Then there are the subsidiary questions: How much development will your shop do? When do you plan to start Java development? Do you intend to develop (create) Java Beans or use (consume) them? How many people will be involved in Java training?

It also makes a difference where people start. A programmer experienced with Java 1.0.x should already understand the basics of AWT and Java programming. Nevertheless, people in this category will need to learn the new event model for Java 1.1 plus the new features that may be germane to a particular project, for example, security, Remote Method Invocation (RMI), etc. Developing Java Beans is new for everyone.

To understand how to get the most out of Java training, it is important to realize that different people learn things differently. There are three fundamental learning styles:

1. Some people learn by observing example behaviors or by reading (visual learners).
2. Some people learn by listening to explanations and directions (auditory learners).
3. Others learn by involvement or doing (kinesthetic learners).

In actuality, most people use a variety of styles but tend to favor one over the other two. When we teach Java, we try to use a variety of techniques to make sure we cover the material in a suitable way for the attendees. You should look for training that includes lecture, written examples, and hands-on practice.

WHAT'S AVAILABLE

Like most popular desktop programming languages, there are a plenty of educational materials available. Without looking very hard you can find books and CBT (computer-based training), including various mass market "multimedia" titles. On the Internet, you will find Java technical specifications, "distance learning," and newsgroups. If you look harder, you can find various courses at training centers (including some colleges, universities, and specialized companies).

While there are a plethora of titles and courses, there's still one problem—the language is evolving faster than the books and course materials. Sometimes publishers will encourage authors to mention something about new features and then the publisher will claim the book covers the new material. This means you must be careful as you evaluate materials and courses. For example, the cover of one recently published self-teaching Java book labeled a "professional edition" suggests that it "Covers Java 1.1." If you purchased the book expecting explanation of the latest Java version, you would be disappointed. The event model demonstrated in the sample code uses the 1.0.x model (switch/case); the 1.1 model (Listener) is discussed, but there are no examples.

One of the things most programmers love is source-code, lots of source-code. They'll use the source code to help them develop Java applications. If code is the primary objective, there is lots of it on the Net and in various books—some good and some not so good. An experienced programmer with a good background in OO should be able to distinguish between the two. Other people won't be so lucky. How will you know the difference? No guarantees. Start by asking questions—listen to people you trust.

HOW TO MAKE IT WORK

I've worked with various organizations to help them learn Java and Object-Oriented programming. I start with a bias that suggests total immersion in Java with a guide/mentor/coach is an important element of success. The suggested mental model for training is very similar to an apprenticeship. After working with many organizations, I've found the following four approaches are shared among the successful Java training efforts:

1. *Have a plan for training.* This is critical. This is part of the answer to the fundamental question I raised above (What is the purpose of Java training?). You must know the outcome you expect from the training. The objective for training should be to find an efficient way to shorten the learning curve for a *small* number of people. Start with a project team of 6 or 7 people at most. Make sure the people who will attend the training (a) want to be there, (b) are relatively homogeneous in their skills and "starting point," and (c) can work together as a group. The plan should include classroom and follow-up: if there are problems or questions that occur after the class, the attendees will need to be able to get answers.

226   LESSONS LEARNED

The ideal situation uses a work-related problem as the source for classroom exercises. It doesn't have to be a specific problem the company wants solved. It is very important that the people attending the training not get caught up in the example; they must be able to keep an open mind to the new concepts and not get hung up on the problem domain details.

As part of your plan, include selecting a training vendor. Make sure the vendor understands your business and is capable and willing to work with you to make the examples and exercises relevant. For example, if your company does not have an inventory, your people don't need to spend time learning patterns that will help them solve inventory problems.

It is best if you plan the training to take place "off-campus" and sans beepers. That way, the attendees will be able to devote 100% of their attention to learning.

2. *Set realistic expectations.* No matter how good your people might be, training does not manufacture overnight gurus. What good training should do is shorten the learning curve. Do not expect the attendees to be overnight wizards. It is entirely possible that some of their early efforts will be candidates for the Java Junkyard. That's OK and is part of the process. Give them time to work with Java, to assimilate the classroom experience so that it becomes second nature.

There is another related problem. Put them to work using Java immediately following the training. Do not expect to send them to class today and then give them their first implementation project 2 months from now. The results will probably be unsatisfactory.

One observation might be helpful. The guru(s) for procedural development might not become the object guru(s). This can sometimes be difficult for both individuals and companies to acknowledge and accept.

3. *Get and use collateral material.* Get recommendations from the course providers for additional supplemental material; browse books in a book store; seek recommendations from people you trust. Get URLs of valuable Java sites (documentation, source code relevant to your organization, etc.), read *Java Report.* The key idea is to have materials that can supplement the workshop learning experience (pre-workshop or post-workshop). This is an on-going process. Today's educational materials (books, etc.) won't necessarily be sufficient for more than a Web year, two tops.

4. *Challenge the attendees to approach the learning process as if they will be responsible to teach the material to someone else when they return from the training.* I'm not suggesting that you can or should actually do this. The chal-

JAVA TRAINING WITHOUT GETTING SOAKED 227

lenge changes the mental set of the attendees. It helps them focus not only on what they do not understand, but what someone back at the office might find difficult, too. The old adage: "Those who can, do; those who can't teach," is wrong. If you really want to learn something, put yourself in the position of having to teach or mentor someone else.

A corollary to this approach—the best teachers are people who have actually implemented real-world projects. As you look for Java course vendors, look for people with experience doing it who can also teach. Part of the learning process requires making mistakes. It is much easier for someone with experience to spot and guide attendees past theses challenges.

MYTHS OF LEARNING JAVA

With the preceding as background to what makes Java training work, what follows is my top ten list of myths about Java training. The people and organizations that share the beliefs expressed in even one of these statements are likely to ignore the four steps I believe are important to make Java training successful.

I picked up an interactive course and a book, isn't that enough? For some individuals this might be sufficient. However, these folks already are quite proficient Java and OO programmers and are looking for the new "stuff" (my favorite polymorphic word). For everyone else, this approach rarely works. If you're learning Java, you will need to ask questions and get immediate feedback. Most people need to be able to explore not only correct practice, but be allowed to make mistakes (preferably in a controlled or classroom environment).

We'll train everyone so that we know what Java is about. When one organization said "everyone," they meant everyone. I'm still not sure I understand why the folks in the telemarketing department needed Java training. To another group, "everyone" meant the entire 300 person development staff— even though only 6 or 7 people would initially be writing Java. If you're going to train everyone, stagger the training so it immediately precedes the individual's need. Don't do it today in anticipation that they *might* need it.

It's just another language; my people pick them up quickly. This is also Microsoft's approach to Java. Nice idea, but it isn't completely true. Yes, Java includes a language, but it doesn't stop there. Java provides a platform-neutral virtual machine that includes many facilities commonly found

228 LESSONS LEARNED

in operating systems—for example: security, memory management, and concurrency (threads). Java is designed for client/server environments that make it ideal for Intra/Internet.

We've been building components in ActiveX so we'll build them in Java, What's the difference? Java and ActiveX are not the same. ActiveX is Microsoft's name for what could be called legacy technologies that used to be called OLE, DDE, and OCX. The technologies pre-date Java and Internet popularity. ActiveX does not have an internal security model nor do ActiveX components execute within a "sandbox." I've heard some well-known consulting firms suggest that there is no difference between Java and ActiveX at the client end. Nothing could be further from the truth. Among other things, Java is secure and free from the most common class of errors (memory management). In addition, today, ActiveX components will only run on Windows; Java is cross-platform.

There aren't enough tools to make Java practical for my people. This one, and the next, are two sides of the same coin. Both serve as illustrations that some people are never happy. There are tools that work with Java, from a variety of vendors including Borland (JBuilder), IBM (Visual Age Java), Microsoft (Visual J++), Sun (Java Studio and Java Workshop), Rational (JFactory), Symantec (Cafe), and others.

There are plenty of tools, but nothing of any value. The thing I found interesting is that the people who make this claim were using visual tools for C++ from one of the vendors listed in the previous myth. The same people who didn't like the Java versions of their favorite tools would not part with the C++ counterpart.

Java programmers are a dime a dozen—we'll just buy what we need. This is not quite a true statement. Java programmers cost much more! Contract help can be even more costly. If you buy contract help, when the contract is complete the expertise leaves with the contractors—that seriously raises the cost of development. If you decided to hire full-time Java employees, you might be surprised to discover that in some areas of the United States the advertisements for Java programmers suggest a premium of anywhere from $10,000 to $40,000 over corresponding C++ programmers. That price tag might make you think twice.

Java is all hype; there's no reason to learn the language since there's no substance to it. There is little anyone can say to these folks. In many cases they also believe that object-oriented programming is "just a passing fad," (that is, about 30 years old, but who is counting).

Java is close enough to C++ that my people won't have any problems. It is true that Java syntax is modeled after C++. The similarity ends there. Java is more than a language. It also includes an event model, remote method invocation, security, threads, and database access, and it is designed for network and client/server environments. Learning Java is more than learning a language. It also requires learning an object-oriented class library, an event model, and more. If you want to build components (Java Beans) then you also deal with a standard interface. In short, while knowing C++ might be helpful, I have not found it to be enough to predict learning-curve time.

You mean they can download the JDK—for free? That's all they need! Absolutely true, the Java Developer's Kit is available for free over the net. However, so is GNU C++ and no one suggests that merely having the compiler is sufficient to learn C++. Consider the Java Developer's Kit a specification. It might be necessary for beginning to develop Java applications (including applets)—I do not consider it sufficient.

SUMMARY

A few years ago, I was teaching a workshop that was based on a book I had written. We'd presented the workshop maybe a dozen times to outstanding reviews. Then one day I got a phone call from a potential attendee who wanted to know what was in the workshop that wasn't in the book. I told him that the workshops were customized to fit the needs of the attendees—to address their specific problems. That wasn't enough. When I told him he could ask questions at the workshop, he told me that wasn't sufficient either.

He wanted the material that I had "withheld" from the book just for the workshops. The fact that I hadn't planned to do workshops based on the book was irrelevant to him. He was only interested in attending if there was "significant" new material that would be "revealed" only to workshop attendees. He didn't care about questions or the synergism of problem solving in a group environment. In almost 15 years of working with clients, this person, thankfully, is the only person I have ever encountered with such a negative bias against training. Without the "hidden" material, the book was sufficient for him; anything else was irrelevant.

This may be true for some people. For most others, working in a structured environment with a mentor who understands Java and what you're trying to accomplish is worthwhile. If you're familiar with Java 1.0.x, you have a leg up on folks that haven't looked at Java—yet. However, there is enough that is new to challenge most people.

Find mentors or coaches that have been there and done that. Look for courses that match the needs you have. Some vendors will work with you to customize the course to fit the specific needs of your people (at the very least the exercises and object patterns should be relevant to your business). Given that Java is less than 2 years old and is still rapidly evolving, it is important to understand that a commitment to Java represents a commitment to continuous learning.

David Moskowitz is president of Productivity Solutions Inc., a Norristown, PA–based skills-transfer consulting firm that specializes in helping its clients deal with new and emerging technology. Contact him at davidm2@usa.net or 76701.100@compuserve.com.